THE PEOPLE EQUATION

THE
PEOPLE
EQUATION

WHY INNOVATION IS **PEOPLE,** NOT PRODUCTS

DEBORAH PERRY PISCIONE
WITH **DAVID CRAWLEY**

BK

Berrett–Koehler Publishers, Inc.
a BK Business book

BERRETT-KOEHLER PUBLISHERS, INC.
1333 Broadway, Suite 1000, Oakland, CA 94612-1921
Tel: (510) 817-2277   Fax: (510) 817-2278   www.bkconnection.com

ORDERING INFORMATION

QUANTITY SALES. Special discounts are available on quantity purchases by corporations, associations, and others. For details, contact the "Special Sales Department" at the Berrett-Koehler address above.

INDIVIDUAL SALES. Berrett-Koehler publications are available through most bookstores. They can also be ordered directly from Berrett-Koehler:
Tel: (800) 929-2929; Fax: (802) 864-7626; www.bkconnection.com

ORDERS FOR COLLEGE TEXTBOOK/COURSE ADOPTION USE. Please contact Berrett-Koehler: Tel: (800) 929-2929; Fax: (802) 864-7626.

Orders by U.S. trade bookstores and wholesalers. Please contact Ingram Publisher Services, Tel: (800) 509-4887; Fax: (800) 838-1149; E-mail: customer.service@ingrampublisherservices.com; or visit www.ingrampublisherservices.com/Ordering for details about electronic ordering.

Berrett-Koehler and the BK logo are registered trademarks of Berrett-Koehler Publishers, Inc.

Printed in the United States of America

Berrett-Koehler books are printed on long-lasting acid-free paper. When it is available, we choose paper that has been manufactured by environmentally responsible processes. These may include using trees grown in sustainable forests, incorporating recycled paper, minimizing chlorine in bleaching, or recycling the energy produced at the paper mill.

Library of Congress Cataloging-in-Publication Data
Names: Piscione, Deborah Perry, author. | Crawley, David, author.
Title: The people equation : why innovation is people not products / Deborah Perry Piscione with David Crawley.
Description: First Edition. | Oakland : Berrett-Koehler Publishers, [2017]
Identifiers: LCCN 2016050068 | ISBN 9781626566415 (hardcover)
Subjects: LCSH: Organizational change. | Corporate culture.
Classification: LCC HD58.8 .P55 2017 | DDC 658.4/063--dc23
LC record available at https://lccn.loc.gov/2016050068

First Edition

22 21 20 19 18 17   10 9 8 7 6 5 4 3 2 1

Cover design: Wes Youssi, M.80 Design. Book production and interior design: VJB/Scribe. Copyeditor: John Pierce. Proofreader: Nancy Bell. Indexer: Theresa Duran. Photos: Pages vii, 94, 120 by David Crawley; page 80 by Shutterstock; page 108 by iStockPhoto; page 130 by Asa Masat; page 144 by Germaine Watkins; page 180 by Dean Duboković. Cartoon page 60 by Manu Cornu. Illustrations pages 22, 40: Janina Lamb.

To our respective families, who inspire us to think differently every morning: Dino, Dominick, Drake, Dayne Alexandria, Suzana, and Katarina.

CONTENTS

Are you trying to get into the first-class cabin, or are you trying to make the train go faster?

WHY PEOPLE MATTER

What type of organization are you part of? Are you in an organization in which everyone is trying to get into the first-class cabin or one where everyone is trying to make the train go faster? The question may seem trivial, but is emblematic of the shift we are going through within our organizations, and perhaps the world at large. Are we going to live in a world of tension between the haves versus the have nots, those who command and those whom are commanded? Or are we going to live in a world where we move forward together? The query illuminates the dichotomy between those who are motivated by power, greed, and control versus those who want to bring forth new thinking. Those in the latter group believe that we should democratize the opportunity for people to bring forth new thinking, new ideas and audacious innovations. The type of organization that they build holds people paramount. Its processes are set up to support, nurture, and provide psychological safety, enabling the organization to leverage all of the talents, passions and interests of their people. In this book, we advocate for a people-centric organization, where rather than trying to focus on getting a first-class ticket, everyone works together to try to make the train go faster.

Organizations and the People Equation

Imagine being the manager who has to look into the eyes of an employee that he or she has worked with for years and tell that employee that his or her job has been eliminated, that they are no longer required, and that their working future has been thrown into disarray. Envision this happening in a world where 45 percent of the people you work with have been replaced by automation. That is the percentage of jobs that McKinsey & Company estimates could be displaced by currently available automation technology.[1]

Given this prospect, where millions will have their jobs displaced, why is it that we are so optimistic about the future? Why do we think that the world will offer more fulfilling work, not less? In the future, the uniquely human capability of innovation will consume more of our work lives. And what's more, because the world is changing faster than ever, the need to innovate will be greater, not less than today; the speed with which companies have to innovate will increase not decrease; and the number of people that companies will need in innovative roles will be greater than they are today. In this future society, companies will have to adapt to harness the passions and interests that drive their people.

However, because the modern hierarchical company is organized principally to get many tasks done, rather than to generate new thinking, companies will have to organize differently—they will have to have different business processes and a different mindset about how they treat their people. It is certain that companies that are not able to change the way they operate will disappear, just like companies that failed to make the leap during other periods of rapid change.

WHERE OUR OBSESSION WITH THE
ORGANIZATIONAL PYRAMID COMES FROM

In 1911, during the later stages of the industrial revolution, Frederick Winslow Taylor, a mechanical engineer who had a passion for organizational efficiency, published *The Principles of Scientific Management.*[2] His book encouraged managers to think of their employees as specialized, replaceable components, like cogs on a wheel. By studying processes and the way people spend time, Taylor created *Taylorism*, an approach by which managers could "secure the maximum prosperity for the employer."[3] Treating employees like a capital asset had a certain attraction, as it provided a clear role for management. In the mass-production era, where the principal method of doing more revolved around deploying more capital and more bodies, Taylorism seemed to fit the world that executives envisioned. Taylorism paid little attention to the thoughts, feelings, and desires of employees, and set the tone of American management practice for the better part of a century and beyond.

At the time, Taylorism was a fantastically successful model, in part because it caused fear—anxiety over losing one's job is a powerful motivation to get things done. Yet in 1924–32, the National Research Council conducted the Hawthorne Experiments, countering Taylorism and asserting that workers are not just machines but people who have feelings and motivations, where wages were just one piece of the pie that encouraged workers to give their best. But despite this new insight, many companies maintained a classic command-and-control structure.

QUALITY IS JOY AT WORK

In 1950, W. Edwards Deming, an engineer and management consultant, addressed the Union of Japanese Scientists and Engineers and preached the concept of "quality management," where the basic principle is that profit comes from repeat customers.

Therefore, employees should concentrate on making the best possible product instead of focusing on management-mandated sales quotas. Deming's concept that "quality is joy at work" implied that productivity would increase when individuals' thoughts, feelings, and desires were respected and taken into consideration. It is perhaps an accident of history that Deming spent most of his career improving Japanese industry as part of post–World War II reconstruction. Simultaneously, in America, Marvin Bower, of the management consulting firm McKinsey & Company, lamented the difficulty of enabling alternatives to traditional hierarchical models.

But despite the fact that many of the underlying assumptions of Taylorism have been thoroughly debunked, it remains an organizing standard that has proved difficult to change. Those who lead hierarchies are more likely to stick with habitual convention and the command-and-control processes of twentieth-century management. In some industries, when the specialized cogs—people—in an organization have been tuned to the needs of a precise business topic, those businesses can run rather well, but only when serving the needs of that particular business process. This means that the hierarchical, fear-oriented, and control-based organization can maintain its position because it can execute on what it does right now. But the world has changed.

THE FLUID ECONOMY:
FROM THE LINEAR TO THE EXPONENTIAL

Just as the variability and abundance of the world today was likely implausible a thousand, a hundred, or even twenty years ago, the future of the world will be inconceivably more fluid and more dynamic than the world we know today. In this book, we describe this pace of rapid change—or perhaps even constant disruption—as "the fluid economy."

Research on the nature of corporate growth indicates that its primary driver is expansion into new and growing markets rather than the market share growth of core markets.[4] In the fluid economy, where every economic domain is ripe for disruption, sustaining a company in the long run requires continually claiming new economic domains.

There is now a considerable disconnection between traditional pyramid-management style and an innovation economy with knowledge workers. By definition, knowledge workers have knowledge that management doesn't and are usually employed to generate new wisdom—making this wisdom useful for the company. Therefore, management must inspire the organization to move to new, often uncharted territory, where people have to be treated better than as cogs in a machine.

As we move from linear to exponential speed in technological advancement, it's clear that the type of work that people do will change. Individuals such as IDEO CEO Tim Brown and University of Michigan professor Jeffrey Liker have started to discuss some of the organizational requirements needed to respond to rapid change and have proposed tactics for doing so.[5] In this fluid economy, having capable, intelligent people who respond quickly to changes in the marketplace is going to be more important than having carved out a market. In a world where information flows freely and start-ups can be formed at practically no cost, it is much easier for an upstart competitor to disrupt whatever market you think you own.

WHY GROWTH IS HARD TO ACHIEVE

Surveys of senior executives by McKinsey & Company indicate that the growth of an organization remains the preeminent challenge, often ranking higher than the combination of many other considerations, such as strategic planning, operational effectiveness, and marketing and branding.[6] This same research indicates that companies that prioritize innovation are able to grow, innovate better, and generate superior shareholder returns. In addition, companies with superior returns are not only better able to return money to shareholders, they are better able to invest in employee support and satisfaction. This difference in company performance and the consequent ability to compensate workers is so pronounced that it has been used by Jason Furman of the President's Council of Economic Advisers and Peter Orszag, nonresident senior fellow at the Brookings Institution, to explain most of the much-storied increases in the income-inequality gap of the last thirty years.[7] Finally, only a small number of companies manage to generate significant revenue from new businesses, and surveys of senior executives indicate that only 6 percent are satisfied with their company's innovation performance.[8] These facts point to a separation between companies that are innovating, growing, and providing for their employees and those that are not. According to Furman and Orszag, since 1990, the performance of publically traded nonfinancial firms has seen a dramatic improvement relative to the average firm. These top performers—those with a return on invested capital (ROIC),[9] excluding goodwill, in the top 10 percentile—perform ten times better than the median firms, compared with three times better only a few decades ago. So some companies seem to be responding to the world we live in now and genuinely profiting from it. This same dramatic separation is not as pronounced when goodwill is included. Some companies seem to be trying to use mergers and acquisitions to respond to these challenges, but while buying innovation does work, it is not as effective as growing it internally.

The point here is that you can get yourself into a virtuous circle or a vicious one. If you are able to grow and innovate, you'll be able to take better care of your employees and recruit the best talent, which will further help you innovate. If you aren't, your organization is likely doomed to a long, slow decline.

THE WORLD HAS CHANGED, SO WHY HASN'T MANAGEMENT?

The ugly truth is that irrespective of all the great ideas in leadership and business management—about a century's worth of ideas and initiatives—the lasting impact on true revolutionary thinking in general-management practice has been limited. Even initiatives that were dramatically successful at one time, such as the results-only work environment (ROWE) at Best Buy from 2005-12, have often been discarded by the organization that introduced them. Sooner or later, bureaucratic institutions revert back to what they know best—being bureaucratic. It is this autopilot mentality that prohibits organizations from growing. You have to wonder, what is the fear about evolving beyond command and control and allowing people to be more free, creative, and able to bring forth new ideas? An even more nagging question is, why is it so difficult to change?

According to an email exchange with Steve Denning, the author of *The Leader's Guide to Radical Management*:

> Achieving sustainable innovation has thus turned out to be a much more intractable problem than most leaders expected it to be. Hierarchical bureaucracy is not a set of linear mechanisms, that can be improved one-by-one through implementing proven remedial measures.... Hierarchical bureaucracy operates more like an ingeniously morphing virus that steadily adapts itself to, and ultimately defeats, intended fixes and returns to its original state, sometimes more virulent than before.[10]

Denning's view reminds us how we deal with many social, economic, and financial ills in our society: when problems are seemingly gargantuan in nature, they are ostensibly impossible to solve, so we do little about them. A simpleminded metaphor may be when you sign your child up for piano lessons, and after six months you discover that your child is not a much better piano player than when she started. Who do you blame? Do you blame the piano teacher who is highly regarded and has many talented and proficient students under her belt? Do you blame your child for not practicing thirty minutes a day as the teacher instructed? Is the piano out of tune or the keys difficult to stroke?

Is your child not as focused and disciplined as she should be? Do you blame the music that has been selected for your child, which is perhaps too difficult or uninspiring? Or does the time of day when the lessons occur make it difficult for your child to focus? Often, you can identify the problem but have great difficulty in prescribing the appropriate remedy.

The reality is that we are living in a world where automation is going to displace the day to day. We've already mentioned that 45 percent of activities that people are paid to perform could be automated with technologies that are available today. In this world, it is people and their ideas that matter, not execution of the leaders' plan. This calls for a very different organization, where it is the frontline people who are at the center of everything the organization does, not the execution of the will of those high in the hierarchy.

What the Fluid Economy Looks Like

We see a less structured world for those who want to excel, not one that involves going to a traditional school or university and then committing to a company in the hope of rising up through the ranks. The days are over when you could offer someone a paycheck and just expect them to perform. Many in the younger generations now want to make a dent in the universe rather than just earn their pay. Firms that can enable people to be bold can achieve audacious new thinking by tapping into each person's passions, desires, and interests. Firms that show people that there's something in it for them are the firms that will win. But you won't and can't win without providing psychological safety.

The gig economy means that contractors and consumers can now be paired online for services ranging from driving someone to their hotel to developing mathematically sophisticated computer algorithms. The emergence of this type of work requires leveraging all the skills and talents of each individual. We expect that T-shaped people—who offer a vertical, hard skill set such as programming, but who also have a horizontal range of curiosity for exploring other interests, such as marketing, sales, financial forecasting, and customer empathy—will succeed in this more fluid economy. In an Uber-like fashion, a young adult may perform many mini apprenticeships that might be widely unrelated but give them exposure to various skills and let them see things from a different perspective. They would be able to draw on all these skills to make themselves a more rounded individual who is better informed, more engaged, and ultimately more fulfilled.

Just as traditional newspapers were challenged by the advent of online news media, traditional higher education will be challenged by an age of online learning. Schools such as Make School, a San Francisco–based, two-year college replacement program for founders and developers, are helping graduates become ready for growing their own companies—or helping them land programming jobs at Google and other leading companies. Free of debt, Make School students don't pay any tuition but provide 25 percent of their earnings from their first two years out of school. You can make lots of arguments for why kids should go to a traditional four-year college for reasons other than academics, but kids are learning at much faster rates in academics today than they did a decade ago. Additionally, millennials and their younger cohorts of Generation Z are developing interests and passions that let them grow into their authentic selves earlier in life in comparison with previous generations.

As more routine work is performed by computers, the value of people will land less on their hard skills and more on their human skills. Creativity, design thinking, and collaboration will be far more important than where one went to college or what you majored in. In 2020, according to *Inc.* magazine, "the ability to come up with solutions, ideas and responses will be highly sought after and propel you" to become a more valuable asset as a worker or entrepreneur.[11] Cross-cultural competency and social intelligence will be an asset as business will continue to operate on a more global scale.

Why Does the People Equation Matter?

We live in Silicon Valley, the innovation capital of the world, where the region's greatest asset and secret sauce is its people and mindset. Deborah moved to Silicon Valley in 2006 after spending eighteen years in one of the most hierarchical environments in the world, Washington, DC. Working in the halls of Congress and the White House and serving as a television commentator for CNN and other national networks, Deborah learned how to do two things really well: put fear in people (because no one does that better than the people in Washington or in the news media), and divide people into "us" versus "them" so that trust is diminished. People were disposable, and no matter how talented you were, there seemed to be a younger, cheaper version of you.

Within six months of arriving in Silicon Valley, Deborah raised capital and inevitably built out four companies in ten years: BettyConfidential, a content leader in the women's space; Alley to the Valley, a national network of accomplished women that fast-tracks professional opportunities; ChumpGenius, an educational gaming company to help kids learn about twenty-first century STEM skills; and Nobiyo Freshwear, a patent-pending undergarment that manages perspiration stains and odor. Convinced that raising money just by having an investor believe in you would not have happened had she stayed in Washington— given its culture and mindset—Deborah took a leave of absence from her entrepreneurial venture to write *Secrets of Silicon Valley: What Everyone Else Can Learn from the Innovation Capital of the World*.[12] In that book, she scratched the surface of the history behind the value placed on people and why the collaborative mindset remains so rooted today. These were the brilliant foresights of people such as Leland Stanford Sr., founder of Stanford University, who came west from New York during the California Gold Rush in the 1850s. Stanford realized that these daring risttakers who came from around the world didn't have to speak the same language or share common cultures or traditions to have the desire to seek a single goal, figure out how to collaborate, and vastly succeed. Stanford knew extraordinary developments could happen—where anything is possible—once you are free from tradition and hierarchy.

When the Fairchild Semiconductor Corporation was founded in Silicon Valley 1957, the company's eight cofounders believed that an organization's people should be like family. Having great disdain for East Coast hierarchy, the "Traitorous Eight," or the "Fairchildren," as they were know, then promised that they would take the "family" culture to any subsequent company they founded. When times are tough, you don't just lay people off, you figure out how to cut back and take care of your people. Collectively, the Fairchildren later founded new companies, creating more than 130 businesses in Silicon Valley, Intel and Advanced Micro Devices among them. In the late 1990s, Google cofounders Larry Page and Sergey Brin believed in creating a lifestyle workplace, where play and creativity are seminal and one's physical, emotional, and spiritual needs are met at an unprecedented level. Firms such as Google, Netflix, Facebook, and Pixar all have lifestyle workplaces that make them tough to compete with.

Because of this mindset, it is Silicon Valley's people who make the difference between an organization's success and failure. This is why in Silicon Valley an equity stake in the company is awarded to those who participate. Often, people are willing or able to trade short-term compensation for the prospect of long-term wealth. It is the brainpower and mindset of Silicon Valley's people that will continue to change the world's expectations and behaviors—the way we think, interact, and evolve. If you can get the mindset right, most anything is possible.

When you launch an entrepreneurial venture in Silicon Valley, it is as if you have given birth to a baby. A majority of founders stay put long after the company has gone public or been acquired. They are the parents who help raise their baby into adulthood, often after gaining extreme wealth. The very notion of birthing a baby changes everything we know to be true about the context of what it means to lead an organization—it changes the mindset of who you hire to help raise your child and, more importantly, how you treat them.

In the start-up world, the entrepreneurial experience of work runs counter to the traditional firm. It is about acting with the unknowns and not necessarily working toward a planned goal. Even more, it is about fulfilling a passion or about being one's authentic self. Most entrepreneurs begin with a problem they want to solve, an opportunity space to tackle, or an under-addressed need to be met. Sometimes, the drive is "let's explore a really cool thing to do and see what comes out of it," or "let's throw up eight to ten things and see what sticks." In this model, it is not about a job description (for anyone who has worked in a start-up, you know that you wear many, many hats). It is extremely improvisational, like a jazz band ready to change direction or add in new rhythms or beats at any time. Regardless, the idea is to get something out there as soon as possible (before it's ideal for what most would consider ready to launch) and see how quickly the need arises to adjust, tweak, or pivot to what the market tells you. In this model, you are testing an entrepreneurial team's thought process, passion, and authenticity, where things continuously develop and change over time. The strategic focus is an ongoing movement that is open-ended, and as far as people go, hinges on trust, collaboration, and being their best self. It is about creating the future together rather than operating in a dichotomy of "us versus them."

Dr. David Crawley is a British citizen raised in Hong Kong during the 1980s, a semiconductor physicist who graduated from Oxford and Cambridge Universities, a former McKinsey consultant, and an athlete who competed in the Olympic trials in rowing for the 2004 Athens games. David witnessed the rise of Hong Kong to become one of the most (if not the most) dynamic cities of commerce on the earth. David saw firsthand the difference between the successful, free-flowing chaos of free market Hong Kong and the stifling and unsuccessful top-down organization of what was then "communist" China. David has worked for, worked in, and managed organizations of every type, from start-ups to military to large mission-driven not-for-profits to huge hierarchical companies. He was always struck by how easily hierarchies, if incorrectly implemented, could stifle the very creative humanity that we all share, and for years he sought to find a better way that more closely matched the world we will all enter into.

We collaborated on Improvisational Innovation, the methodology that came out of Deborah's time observing Qualcomm's ImpaQT innovation program. Over the years, we have been in numerous conversations with C-suite executives of multibillion-dollar companies who are kept up at night not knowing the future of their company or where the next big idea is. Very often, discussions of innovation with the C-suite devolved into a conversation about the products that the company will release soon, rather than addressing any underlying method by which new ideas get explored or, more importantly, a deep sense of who the people are that work for them. We'd inevitably ask about who in the organization were their great risk takers or entrepreneurial types, and we'd inevitably end up with blank stares. It confirmed our view—innovation and the growth that it brings are the greatest things that these executives lack. Meanwhile, despite the confidence they may or may not have in their team (no matter how large the organization is), they usually cannot clearly articulate who in the organization is there to generate ideas or what the process is by which it occurs.

We are often asked, "Who has done talent development well?" As you read ahead, the answers may not be what you'd typically expect. The stark reality is that we couldn't find strong examples of people-centric organizations within traditional corporate America, and the Googles of the world have been exhaustively researched and documented. Therefore, you will find many case studies that we have gathered from outside corporate America that show what might be possible when a company focuses on the creative energies of its people rather than its hierarchical organizing structure.

We have seen what happens when you organize for control rather than for your people. We've worked in and witnessed other spheres of influence, where greed, money, politics, and control are the driving influences, and we understand that when you are surrounded and ingratiated into those cultures, that is your normal. Organizations are finding that they can't sustain healthy revenues if they are not increasing the speed of innovation. Investments in new technologies or operations do not create innovations—people do.

What unfolds in the next eight chapters is what you need to do in order to adopt the People Equation. These will be the keys to how you transform your organization to put people first, enable them to innovate, and drive the business to success in a fluid economy. We will show you how to create a culture where risk taking is rewarded, mavericks are encouraged, collaboration between highly competent people is nurtured, and, when experiments and new initiatives are proposed, the response is to ask how rather than question why. We are convinced that orienting your organization around the creative energies of your people will enable you to grow and build value more effectively. Just watch how much faster the train can travel!

The People Equation Prescription

The People Equation is simply this: provide a culture where risk taking is encouraged and psychological safety enables people to innovate. This culture consists of four elements:

$$\text{The People Equation} = \text{Psychological Safety} \times \left(\begin{array}{c} \text{Innovation Process} \\ + \\ \text{Inverted Organization} \\ + \\ \text{Mindset} \end{array} \right)$$

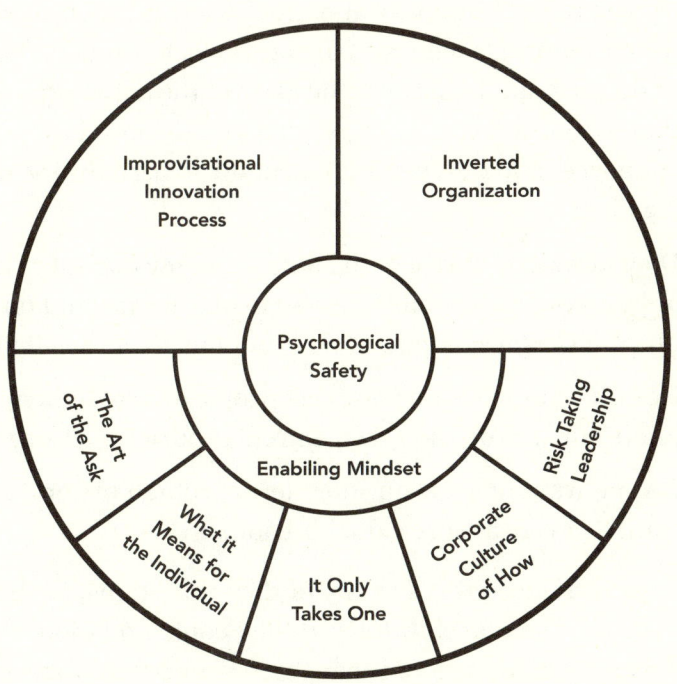

Figure 1: The People Equation Framework

Two states of equilibrium exist today. One is where individual people seem less important than the hierarchy. This is an organization where everyone is trying to get into the first-class cabin of the train. The other state is one in which people and their ideas are more important than the hierarchy. This is an organization in which everyone is working to make the train go faster. The focus on people is greater than the importance of the hierarchy.

THE PEOPLE EQUATION FRAMEWORK

Why do people matter in an increasingly technological and automated world? This is the perplexing question we set out to answer. The People Equation asks you to seek answers to these soul-searching questions:

- Do you want to innovate and grow at a rate constrained by the corporate strategy and the ideas of a few top managers, or do you want to harness the ideas of the entire organization so that you can leverage what's on the minds of your employees and develop incrementally to perhaps the next big idea?

- Do you want to thrive in the fluid economy and take risks, or is it more comfortable for you to play it safe (and possibly observe the company's slow, but inevitable decline)?

- Do you want to retain your best people or watch them jump ship and do their own entrepreneurial start-up?

- Do you want to focus on short-term profitability or do you want to create a more valuable company?

If you've answered yes to any of these questions, we believe that to do an effectual shift toward the People Equation, Figure 1, will require organizational changes in your process, structure, and mindset. In the People Equation, a cerebrally engaged set of people becomes the most important driver of success because there are certain things that only people can do.

Psychological Safety: The Enabler of Innovation

The bedrock of a people-centered institution is one where those in it feel a sense of psychological safety. This is the sense that regardless of what may happen, individuals in the organization will be respected and will not be penalized for honest attempts to improve the organization that perhaps don't work out. Psychological safety is the feeling created when the organization is supportive of taking risks. It is a state of mind that all the individuals in the institution contribute to, and it arrives when the organization makes a conscious choice not to use either explicit or implicit threats as a way to motivate people. When people feel this sense of psychological safety, it unlocks the higher-order thinking that we all possess to lead to more creative and meaningful interactions. In chapter 1, we show that unless you respect the individual and create an environment for psychological safety, the people in that environment cannot be distinctively creative.

Process for Breakout Innovation

In the People Equation, you have to provide a regular innovation process that democratizes participation rates, where anyone in any corner of the company can partake in bold and incremental experiments, irrespective of their age, experience, education, pay grade, and so on. You need a formalized process with a clearly defined time line in which people can share their ideas, passions, and interests in a trusted environment—one that will benefit the company in the short- and long-term and reward individuals as though they were building out their own entrepreneurial venture. As you will read in chapter 2, Improvisational Innovation™ establishes a pipeline that draws in ideas and people from the company itself, and then trains those people and develops the ideas until viable teams emerge that can run these new internal start-ups. These innovative and dynamic teams understand the company but are not bound by its constraints and are empowered to push boundaries to grow the organization. Improvisational Innovation enables growth for the corporation, but is a bottom-up approach that also engages, develops, excites, and retains the company's most valuable employees.

Inverted Organization: Raise Up Your Innovators

If corporations want to be part of the fluid economic future, they must set up other parts of their organization that are oriented toward the needs of their innovators and create the conditions to nurture them to achieve success. As you will find in chapter 3, a devolved organizational structure—what we call the *inverted organization*—will be critical here, as the attempt to control people, as we have seen, is loaded with either explicit or implicit notions of threat. This causes at best disengagement and at worst the active pursuit of a poor idea that was enabled through the superior position of an individual rather than because the best minds were thinking hard about the problem. To get there, senior managers have to embrace the benefits that a people-centric enterprise will bring. They are the ones who must, through devolving power downward or through growing part of the organization to be nonhierarchical, create an organization that is focused on the needs of those on the front line.

A Mindset That Makes the Train Go Faster

The People Equation enables the self-actualization of the employee by helping them build value from their inward or outward passions and interests. Only the organizations that concentrate on the mindset of making the train go faster rather than encouraging people to push their way into the first-class cabin will succeed and win in a fluid economy. You will have a stronger engine for innovation and growth. In this environment, as we detail in chapters 4 and 5, you embrace trust and collaboration and celebrate successes and failures. Reprogramming senior-management behaviors, from control to empowerment, is required. Using a language of "Yes and . . ." rather than "No" will help. Building environments where interpersonal interactions are devoid of explicit or implicit threats, so that people can take measured risks and grow, will result in a workforce that is more capable of tackling the rigors of the fluid economy. In the fluid economy, where there will be a need to respond creatively to rapid changes, we will need risk-taking leaders who can embrace and understand risk and enable others to take risks. As we move into a fluid economy, where more of the routine, automatable processes are and will continue to be taken up by machines, the childlike, creative instinct, accompanied by other uniquely human capacities, will become more central in one's organization's ability to innovate.

A Corporate Culture of How

A Corporate Culture of How is not about what you do but how you get things done. In getting things done, you need to give people time, an environment for them to bring new ideas to the table, and a process to execute. How ideas are improved upon can only happen through taking an idea and allowing other people to build on it. In chapter 5, we discuss what this Corporate Culture of How looks like, the vernacular associated with that culture, and what some of the tools are to create an engaging culture. We recognize that constructing cultural change is hard, and we suggest that if your culture is deeply rooted in bad behaviors, you need to first disrupt the current culture before trying to grow a Corporate Culture of How. We propose some formal mechanisms that may be useful in the construction of a new culture, but we recognize that, as always, the personal leadership qualities of those who head the organization are the decisive factor for a fruitful cultural shift.

It Only Takes One

People respond to other people in unique ways. Sometimes, to move your organization to new heights, what is required is as simple as role modeling. In hierarchical organizations, mavericks often struggle to conform and succeed, yet these mavericks are exactly the type of people you want in your organization if you want novel and creative problems to be solved. In chapter 6, we talk about the impact that these trailblazers can have and suggest that you need to highlight the achievements of these pioneers rather than suppress them.

What It Means for the Individual

In the fluid economy, the front line consists of knowledge workers who drive innovation. In this environment, the frontline worker needs to have the freedom to make innovative decisions that can affect the course of the company's progress. This requires a high degree of personal responsibility and a strong commitment to the success of the organization, and it requires the competence to ensure that these front liners don't let the organization down. Developing your people, and then rewarding them for the groundbreaking or cost-cutting work that they do, becomes critical not because they are motivated by the money but because if you refuse to share the rewards of good work, you devalue them. In chapter 7, we talk about the importance of careful cultivation of the individuals who make up your institution so that it can prosper in the long term.

The Art of the Ask

People are social animals, and for an innovative culture to emerge, people have to engage with other people and build on each other's ideas. Those people need to engage in reflecting about problem solving, opportunity spaces, and underaddressed needs—all contributing their own thoughts, feelings, and desires so that the result is greater than the sum of the parts. It is only when a group of people collectively engage in a culture of possibility that we can innovate at the maximum possible rate. In chapter 8, we discuss the art of collaboration and being cognizant of your ask (*what do you need to bring forth a good idea and execute?*) and your offer (*what can you provide to someone else who may need your support or expertise?*).

Can you think out of the box?

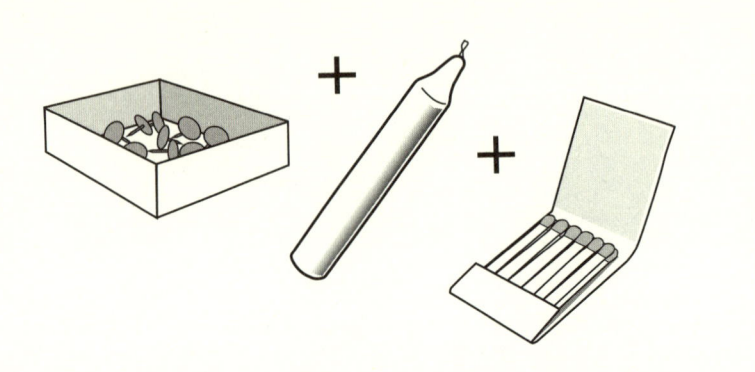

Figure 2a: A book of matches, a box of tacks, and a candle are supplied with the instructions to attach the candle to a corkboard.

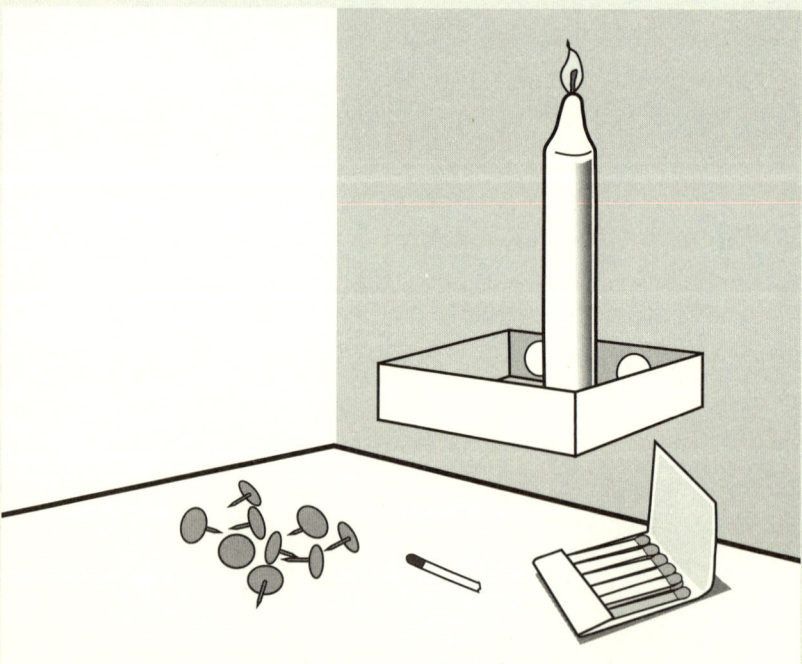

Figure 2b: The solution, which requires out-of-the-box thinking, is to repurpose the box as a candleholder.

CHAPTER 1

THE PSYCHOLOGY OF INNOVATION

The classic experiment on the concept of creative insight is the candle problem (figure 2a and 2b). Proposed by Gestalt psychologist Karl Duncker in his master's thesis in 1926 and published posthumously twenty years later, the experiment involves a box of tacks, a candle, and a book of matches.[1] The test subjects are told to attach the candle to a corkboard by using only the items presented to them. Typically, some subjects try to use the tacks to attach the candle to the corkboard, while others creatively melt some candle wax and attempt to attach the candle to the corkboard with it. Unfortunately, none of these methods work. What does work is to realize that the box that holds the tacks can also be used to hold the candle. In this way, a tack can be used to attach the box to the corkboard and the candle can rest in the box.

The candle problem is a great test of creative insight because to solve it, people have to overcome their preconceived notions of what the box is there for. This is why for ninety years it has been the benchmark for testing this type of psychological capacity and is still actively discussed.

The interesting thing is what it tells us about how the mind works under different stimuli. Classic reasoning from a typical modern-management or Taylorist-management approach is that to get the task done more quickly, one should incentivize the task.

So what happens if you add a small financial incentive to come up with a solution to the candle problem faster?

This was tried by psychologist Sam Glucksberg in 1962. To create baseline times, a small financial reward was offered to one group for solving the candle problem more quickly, while another group was asked to just move as quickly as they could. Surprisingly, the group that was incentivized did the task *more slowly* than the group that wasn't.

There is plenty of evidence to suggest that for straightforward tasks, incentives do work—at least in the short term.[2] Incentives are widely deployed in management, initially for the types of tasks that matter in a mass-production factory or any other Taylorist workplace. Having said that, when creativity or lateral thinking is required, it's not just that incentives don't work; they actually reduce productivity, and this conclusion is supported by a body of scientific literature, starting with Glucksberg's 1962 paper, and continues to be researched to this day.[3] What incentives do is induce stress and create focus or even fear. These things are great when the task is known, but when the task isn't, they are counterproductive. We very much support financial and equity rewards in our innovation process, but we want to emphasize that while stress may make you work faster, it can shut down higher-order thinking. Focus is great for excluding the nonessential, but it also kills lateral thinking. As we will describe in the next section—when we place these effects in an actual, observed corporate environment—stress and fear are often used by people high up in the hierarchy to create action; however, this may not be the type of action that is needed if creative lateral thinking is required to solve the problems that the corporation may face.

This teaches us that what seems intuitively correct, about setting up hierarchical, incentivized systems with vigorous rewards and punishment, is something that worked well for the industrial economy. But transplant those same notions to the fluid economy, where creativity is paramount, and you are setting yourself up for failure. If we want our organizations to be creative and to meet the challenges of the fluid economy, then a typical hierarchical organizing structure with short-term, carrot-and-stick incentives will not work.

The Boardroom Turret Gunner

A few years ago, we witnessed a senior executive meeting on the East Coast in a luxuriously appointed boardroom atop the headquarters of a publicly listed company. We'll protect the company and the time we were there, but it was instantly clear who was in charge. Because the meeting was so contrary to what we encounter in Silicon Valley, we asked ourselves, was it the way the imposing executive sat or where? Was it the fact that everyone in the room oriented their chairs to him? Perhaps it was the way everyone else in the room was restrained while that singular individual barked orders—in addition to the fact that everyone in the room was slightly deferential to him and the amount of airtime he consumed. Perhaps it was the fact that when that individual paused, everyone else waited, or the way the individual swung around in the plush swivel chair in which he sat and fired questions to the prepared and unprepared alike. We referred to this executive as the *turret gunner*; he has all the trappings of a hierarchical leader.

As we sat and watched, somewhat in disbelief at the way the turret gunner was treating his subordinates, we learned that several people in the room spent hours a week working with the turret gunner and knew what was likely to evoke a negative response and what was not, but the person presenting that day was not one of them. The presentation was related to a review of a new initiative, and the turret gunner swung around and pointed his questions to the presenter. The fast-paced questions were laden with either implicit or explicit threats. The explicit threats could be as blunt as, "I'll fire you if you don't . . ." The implicit threats could be as subtle as, "What was the performance of...?" The presenter, who had lived and breathed the project for the last year, knew every detail of how the project functioned but somehow was not able to recall the answers. For the presenter, important details that needed to be brought to the forefront were memories that, in that environment, couldn't be recalled.

The presenter continued talking but couldn't recall information important to the decisions that were being made. The stream of verbiage seemed incoherent, and the senior people, especially the turret gunner, seemed to feel confirmed in their view that they were senior for a reason and the presenter junior for a reason. The presenter seemed to agree to do things that he certainly couldn't execute. He agreed to do things that he wouldn't otherwise do, and in more than one extreme case made commitments and agreed to targets that he should have known were unattainable. Ultimately, the people in the room made a set of decisions about the project, but those decisions were not the ones that could best spur the project forward because the best information was not discussed.

What happened? The harangued presenter wasn't thinking at his best because he experienced an amygdala hijack. The amygdala is a small part of the brain that controls the fight or flight response. In situations in which the amygdala perceives a threat, this tiny part of the brain evokes an emotional response and can respond a few milliseconds faster than the thinking brain, or cerebrum, can. As such, the amygdala will override or hijack higher brain thinking and drive an immediate action-oriented response. This part of the brain is there for our survival in threatening situations, so this response can be powerful and automatic. However, the office environments where most of us spend our days are far removed from the wild environments in which the fight or flight response evolved. What this means is that while in primitive humans, immediate action was required to dispense with an existential threat, in the modern office, those actions might be unhelpful or even preposterous.

An amygdala-oriented response is dangerously seductive precisely because of the immediate, action-oriented response it causes. The tried-and-true management technique of anger and shouting is based on this truth.

In the Royal Military Academy Sandhurst (the British army's officer training academy), which David attended, issuing certain types of commands clearly, loudly, and as an order is a skill that is actually taught. The "do it or you're fired" message, delivered either explicitly or implicitly, is dangerously effective at creating movement. Leaders who make use of it may even feel a sense of satisfaction that they are able to motivate people to take action by using it. However, the question remains: what action? If the action is generated by bypassing the cerebrum, in which the required decision-making faculties are housed, then for the modern people-centric enterprise it can be a disaster. If the business that we are in is one where we require people to think about problems rather than move widgets, then we must strive to create an environment that remains effective even as we move as far away as we can from that type of seductive mode of operation.

Hierarchical organizations are intrinsically designed in this way. In a typical hierarchical organization, action occurs according to who is in the senior position, not who has the best idea. In a hierarchical organization, the senior people can typically fire or at least negatively influence the careers of their subordinates. While the massive negative consequence of a firing is under the control of a manager, promotion beyond a single hierarchical level is usually outside the control of a direct manager. As such, the traditional hierarchy is a fear-based system. The manager can fire, but he or she usually cannot move the person up more than part of a hierarchical level. This type of organization is designed to get an army of things done, by an army of people.

If you think back to the candle problem, when subjects are given an incentive, that is thought to create stress—an amygdala-based response. This shuts down the cerebrum, which is necessary to solve the problem most quickly. In essence, hierarchical organizations are designed to do this in order to create action, but they do so at the expense of creative thinking. So, the effectiveness of the hapless victim of the turret gunner suffers the same effects that cause subjects in the candle problem to slow down.

We must create a people-centric organization that promotes mindfulness and moves far away from the threat-oriented calls to action that are common in hierarchical organizations. The bottom line is that the people-centric organization needs to create an environment in which people feel safe enough to share ideas—but *more than that,* they need to feel safe enough to *have* ideas.

Psychological Safety and What It Means for Your Business

The notion of psychological safety is a well-studied phenomenon.[4] The basic concept is centered on the extent to which people believe their actions will avoid personally negative repercussions. Those repercussions are—very often—subtle, such as a dismissive comment from a superior. It is important to understand that this is distinct from avoiding personal responsibility or accountability. It is simply that honest attempts to do the right thing for the team, even if they are mistaken, are not punished.

Through surveys, it is possible to measure the level of psychological safety, and high levels of psychological safety are correlated with the following:

- Higher rates of learning

- Higher rates of creativity

- Fewer mistakes

- Higher levels of team performance

These studies reveal sometimes surprising results. For example, team environments where mistakes are interpersonally penalized have lower levels of psychological safety and actually result in more mistakes. This occurs even in cases where those mistakes may be very serious. Why? If you are going to be penalized for speaking up, emotionally you will be less likely to do it, even if logically you should. Later in the chapter, we will talk about how nurses don't report medication errors in an environment like this.

RISK-TAKING CULTURES

Silicon Valley is often described as having a risk-taking culture. In many ways, it's probably more accurate to describe it as having a culture that accepts mistakes or a culture of high psychological safety. As the story goes in Silicon Valley, the reason all the office buildings are two stories high and surrounded by grass is that when you feel like throwing yourself out of the top floor, you wind up just spraining an ankle, only to go home and write another business plan. Typically, failing in a business a couple of times is viewed positively in Silicon Valley, and this is a manifestation of an environment of high psychological safety. Certainly, there are people here who are naturally bold risk takers, who have a risk-taking DNA, and they come here because this is an environment where they thrive.

A state of psychological safety is something that most humans are not predisposed to. In the natural environment, one might look into the distance to see an object, and that object may be unclear. It could be a bush laden with tasty berries or it could be a dangerous wild beast. You might be trying to decide whether to investigate the object further. An optimistic assessment of what it is might lead you to a nice snack, but it could also lead to your death. A pessimistic assessment at least ensures that you will survive to forage another day. As such, humans are predisposed to a state of psychological arousal for threats, and it doesn't take much to raise this state of arousal. Human beings are predisposed not to move out of their comfort zone, not to go and do risky things, and to generally like routine.

Fortunately, however, things can be done to counter these tendencies and thus enable greater psychological safety, reduce threat-oriented thinking, and enable more cerebral thinking.

THE PEOPLE-CENTRIC ENVIRONMENT

A people-centric work environment is one that is designed to meet the needs of the people who work in it rather than the needs of the most senior person. The goal is to create an environment in which intrinsic motivations can come to the forefront. So, while financial motivations matter, as we learned earlier in this chapter and discuss further in chapter 5, financial rewards can, if misapplied, be counterproductive. If we are interested in creating a people-centric environment, we need to consider several elements: the physical environment, the mindset, and process.

Physical Environment

If you can, slow down for a moment and imagine a place, somewhere you feel happy, safe, and secure—a place where you are relaxed. It could be by the ocean or in the mountains; somewhere familiar or somewhere new. Look around that place and see all the things that you can see. Follow your eyes to absorb all the beauty around you and imagine hearing all the sounds you might hear in that place. As you read these words, imagine reaching out and touching something around you and running your hands through its physical material. It could be warm sand from a beach, grass in a field, water, or stone. It could be anything that is pleasing to you. As you imagine this place and think about it, does it seem like it's a vacation place? Or does it seem like it's a workplace?

When people go on vacation, they generally choose to go to a place of beauty to unwind, relax, or whatever the term is that causes you to be able to think well and more clearly. Many of us go to a place that is usually free from threats caused by other people, a place where there are few demands of us and where we are free to create demands for ourselves. For us and our colleagues who write, retreating to a place like this is often where we are most productive, where we have the greatest capacity for creative thought. It is as if the cerebrum can be most fully engaged.

But what if your workplace was like that? Most of us spend our days in an environment characterized by gray walls at right angles to each other, but not all work environments are like that. Here in Silicon Valley, there are workplaces that are eons apart from the towering cube-farms one finds in many of our larger cities. Some of these workplaces have a lot more in common with a resort vacation village. The Googles, Facebooks, and Pixars of the world do a phenomenal job replicating the resort lifestyle in the workplace.

The Mindset

The fundamental mindset of the people-centric organization is one of psychological safety. This does not mean a lack of accountability, but it does mean that honest attempts to do something different are rewarded rather than punished. There are several areas where people are typically vulnerable and are exposed. In particular, these are areas where a mindset of reward is important:

- Feedback seeking
- Help seeking
- Innovation
- Boundary spanning
- Speaking up about concerns / Providing feedback

Feedback seeking is the process through which people try to get information about their own individual performance in order to improve it. It is almost always a vulnerable place to be because you are explicitly asking for things that you might have done wrong and need to improve on. Feedback seeking can be difficult for the ego, but it is vital to be able to grow and develop into a more effective person. It is something that has to be encouraged in an organization that wants to see people who are more effective than they once were.

Help seeking, where one seeks out assistance, always includes, either explicitly or implicitly, the admission that you can't do the task yourself. While it is a vulnerable place to be, failure to engage in help-seeking behavior means that the corporation will rarely be getting the best person on the job to engage. When there is the sense that exposing this vulnerability will lead to negative repercussions, people stop doing it—and the organization suffers.

Innovation by definition is a process where you try to do something new. It is always fraught with difficulty because there can be no certainty as to whether the new and innovative idea will actually work—if that were known, it would not be innovation. This makes innovation a precarious business. It is frequently expensive and, if you are being truly innovative, must sometimes result in failure. It is often impossible to affirmatively defend an innovative idea as good because there is no data yet to support that view. If you are innovating, you are exposed. When there is a sense that this exposure will lead to negative repercussions, people stop trying to innovate, and that is disastrous for the long-term health of the company. Innovation will be the lifeblood of all companies in the fluid economy and is a prerequisite for growth.

Boundary spanning is about the cross-functional interaction needed to deal with a complex corporate problem. The people in your own group don't have the right expertise, for example, or perhaps they have just run out of ideas. It's the type of problem for which you gather all the best experts from as many different backgrounds as you can find in a single room. This type of interaction, where you force individuals to work across typical organization silos, is important for solving problems that either are complex or need added creativity to solve. In a people-centric enterprise, cross-functional interaction is vital to bring the best minds to bear on a complex, multidimensional problem. It is also important because cross-functional interaction is frequently where the greatest creative energy can be found. Yet this always involves an element of vulnerability. By definition, the people that you work with in boundary-spanning activities have to be people that you know less well, and it is not a natural thing to reach out to people who are unknown to you, nor is it even always possible. Unless there is a mindset that a cross-functional approach is preferable in a lot of ways to reaching out to those within your own silo, then you will limit the opportunity to creatively solve problems. In a people-centric organization, the belief that boundary spanning is not only desirable but welcome.

Speaking up about concerns and **providing feedback** can sometimes save lives. Medical environments are fraught with the possibility of dangerous mistakes. If the environment is not centered on people, the rates of errors increase. Studies involving nurses have indicated that medical teams with high levels of psychological safety tend to make fewer medication errors.[6] Why? On those teams, nurses feel that they are able to point out potential medication errors to more senior staff. Contrast this with teams that are more hierarchical. On those teams, speaking up could elicit dismissive and negative comments from more senior staff. The result is that nurses are less willing to point out medication errors unless they are very certain they are about to occur. It is not merely that a potentially life-saving comment from a nurse is heard and ignored; it is that, after a while, those comments aren't even made.

The People Equation Prescription

Getting to Psychological Safety

What are some of the things that enable a sense of psychological safety? Well, according to modern research, five things are known to enhance feelings of psychological safety:[5]

- Use of practice fields
- Team leader behavior
- Group dynamics
- Trust and respect
- Supportive organizational context

Use of practice fields.   Alex Honnold is widely regarded as one of the most talented free-solo climbers in the world. He is known for making long, high-commitment climbs up practically sheer rock walls without ropes. Hanging from your fingertips on an overhang five hundred feet up would, for most people, be terrifying. However, Alex doesn't describe it that way: "The moment you get scared it's a negative spiral," he mentioned in a 2015 interview.[7] "Once you lose control you get freaked out, then you get shaky, then you *should* be scared because you won't be able to climb as well. Then you make a mistake, and mistakes are costly. The key is to keep those thoughts away; just climb."[8]

Alex has clearly found a way to control his feelings of fear in an otherwise terrifying situation. He practiced climbing almost exclusively indoors for eight years before he started to focus on outdoor climbing. Today, before he does any of the long free-solo routes he's famous for, he typically practices the route a dozen times or more with ropes. In short, Alex has found ways to practice the route over and over so that when it comes time for him to free-solo the route, he can do so without fear.

The use of practice fields is as useful in business as it is in climbing—it is the act of creating a risk-free environment in which to practice an activity so that it can be done with high levels of psychological safety. Airline pilots use simulators, and army platoons use military exercises. Even McKinsey & Company makes use of practice fields—all their consultants routinely run through theoretical client-engagement scenarios in training. Practice fields enable you to adapt mentally to the scenario that you are about to encounter and lessen the fear response, which, as we have discussed, can override higher brain functions, leading to disaster.

Team-leader behavior.   It is well known that the behavior of the team leader sets the tone for the entire organization; so, too, with psychological safety. Team leaders create a safe example for others to follow and thus are always an important lever for influencing the behavior of a group. The research shows that when team leaders themselves exemplify behaviors that represent psychological safety, the rest of the group follows suit.[7] The extent to which the team leader does or does not stigmatize those who make honest mistakes, the extent that the team leader discusses how mistakes are inevitable and that what is required is open discussion about them, or the extent to which team leaders discuss their own mistakes and vulnerabilities will drive the level of psychological safety the team experiences. Furthermore, team leaders are in a position to monitor formal and informal group dynamics, set up practice fields, and engage in other practices known to promote psychological safety.

Deliberate group dynamics.   Have you ever worked in a group where one person played the role of a "jester," continually making fun of a situation? Perhaps you've worked with an individual who frequently injected negative and critical remarks in group discussions. People tend to take on roles in an organizational context, and those roles may be different from the roles they have outside work. Very often, these roles are informal and are dependent on how the individuals in the group interact. Group dynamics are infectious, and these group dynamics can be either supportive or destructive of trust. Formalizing or discussing group dynamics is one method to ensure that a dynamic exists that is supportive of high levels of psychological safety. For many years, David worked at McKinsey, where new teams are assembled for each new client project. At the beginning of a new project, the team sits down together and explicitly discusses the working styles of all the individuals on that team so that the individuals on the team can accommodate differences in a way that avoids unnecessary criticism. Standardizing certain types of interaction can also help to create the right type of dynamic.

In the military, interactions are highly standardized. The way in which an officer gives orders to his troops follows a prescribed format. The thinking methods that officers use to develop and write those orders follow a standard method that is understood by all officers. The roles of individuals in a fighting unit are standardized and known. The result is that when you place an officer within a new unit, that officer is able to command the unit in a standardized way that is understood by everyone, even if they haven't worked together before.

Similarly, some organizations, such as Toyota, have a standardized way of solving problems. This means that when people from across the organization understand each other, they can effectively work without unnecessary criticism. The Toyota Code of Conduct is a rather short, eighteen-page document that describes what is required from every employee. Toyota uses the term *trust* no less than twenty times in this document, and with good reason. "Mutual Trust and Mutual Responsibility" is a core value at Toyota, one that is recognized as critical to the long-term success of the company. When there is genuine trust earned through repeated positive interactions, with credible people who have the interests of others at heart, then it allows you to feel safe in dealing with that person and the entire organization. Everyone working to continually build trust is a requirement and, once that trust is established, amazing things are possible.

From the outside, Toyota may seem hierarchical, but inside, the company in many ways embodies frontline empowerment. Factory production-line workers have within arms reach a cord that they can pull to stop the production line until a problem they have identified is resolved. Toyota has turned the hierarchy on its head. Normally, it would be the factory manager who had the power to force all the resources in the factory to address a problem that he thought was important. At Toyota, it's the front-line employee who can cause all the work in the factory to stop until his or her issue is resolved. The result is that problems get resolved quickly—most pulls of the cord get released within seconds of them happening. This system both requires and enables extraordinary levels of trust. Frontline employees are trusted to highlight important quality problems, and managers are trusted to solve them. Not only is Toyota the largest car company in the world, it is also, by some measures, the most profitable. In each segment of the auto market that it competes in, Toyota has the highest gross margin. Routinely, their personnel turnover rates are among the lowest in any region where they hire. But more important than this, cultivating an attitude of mutual trust and respect is in some ways the definition of an environment where psychological safety can flourish.

When everyone is engaged in building trust, that creates a foundation where there is no need to attack someone for poor performance, second-guess, or engage in other activities that tend to undermine psychological safety. Most importantly, psychological safety permits respect for the individual—the notion that regardless of their needs or quirks, they are valuable and should be treated as such. When mutual trust and respect for the individual are present, they are a self-reinforcing pair that enables an attitude of psychological safety to exist and further business success.

Supportive Organizational Context.   David is 6' 9" and can recall a time when he was a junior officer in the army: "They couldn't get me a piece of dress uniform my size. I escalated all the way to brigade command and still there was no satisfactory response."

David tried scrounging kit and equipment stores, but this also proved futile and required a lot of effort over many months. He recalls how it made him feel: "Well, if they couldn't get me a few pieces of cloth when I am working on a military base, then what hope do they have in getting some other piece of equipment I might need when, perhaps, I might be in the field?"

The failure of the organization in a small way led to a sense that the organization *couldn't* help him, perhaps when he might desperately need it. The notion of whether the organization can provide for the individual is linked to the notion of psychological safety. After all, it's difficult to feel a sense of security when you also feel like the organization may not be able to provide the things you need to be secure. As such, ideas of psychological safety are tied to the capacity of the organization to provide for each individual within it.

Human beings are animals that are only a stone's throw away from ancestors who lived in an environment where danger was everywhere. Humans evolved a capability to instantly recognize risk and shut down all brain functions that are not essential to dealing with that threat. This adaptation was vital for survival when human beings mostly lived in wild spaces, but in a knowledge-driven, fluid economy, this adaptation is problematic because it leads to shutting down the very part of the brain that needs to be functioning to come up with creative solutions. A people-centric enterprise can create an environment of high psychological safety and thus enable the individuals that work within it to engage all of their mental faculties for a more satisfying and successful organization.

Do you have a method to make innovation happen?

THE IMPROVISATIONAL INNOVATION PROCESS

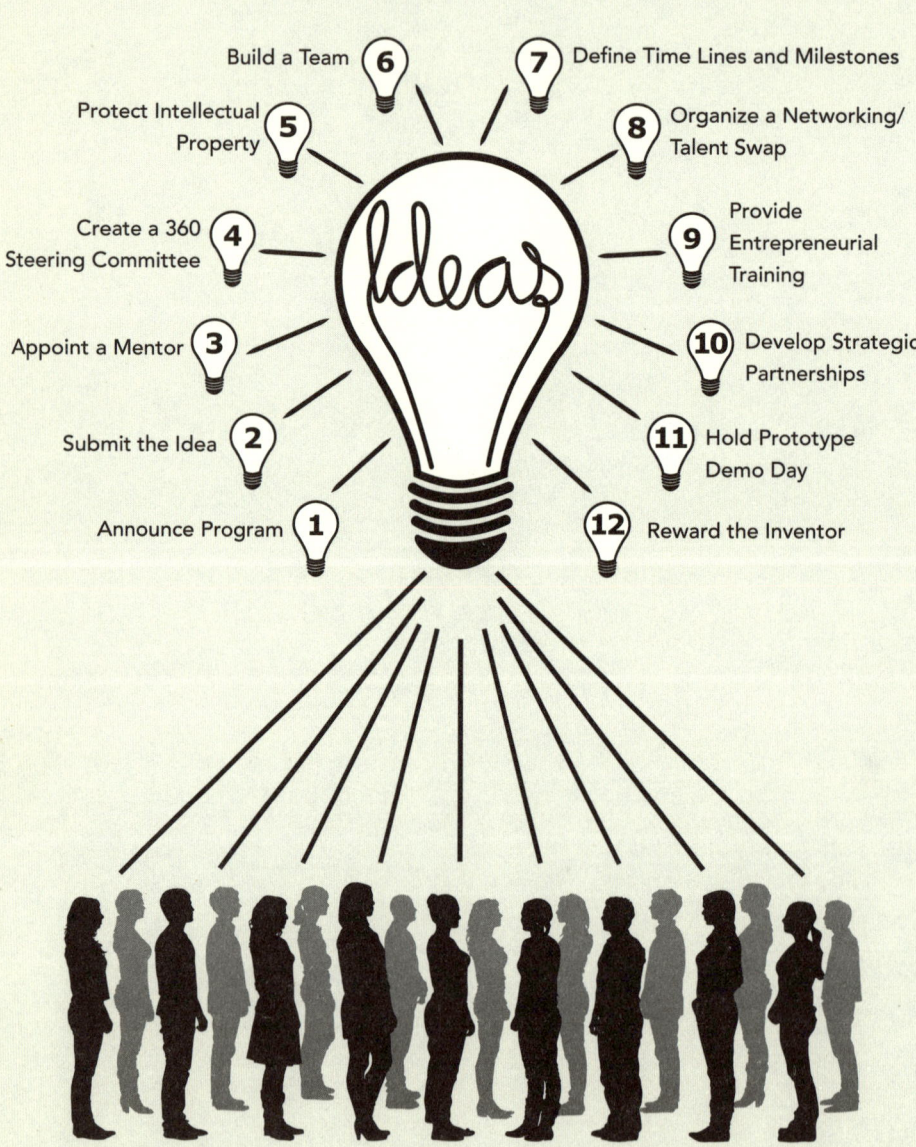

Build a Team **6**

7 Define Time Lines and Milestones

Protect Intellectual Property **5**

8 Organize a Networking/ Talent Swap

Create a 360 Steering Committee **4**

9 Provide Entrepreneurial Training

Appoint a Mentor **3**

10 Develop Strategic Partnerships

Submit the Idea **2**

11 Hold Prototype Demo Day

Announce Program **1**

12 Reward the Inventor

CHAPTER 2

THE PROCESS: IMPROVISATIONAL INNOVATION

Pat Younge, former chief creative officer at the BBC, was looking to find ways to generate ideas for programs that would better connect across generational differences and cohorts in the United Kingdom. The BBC had operated much the same way for eighty years, but with the advancement of technology and introduction of social media, audience behaviors had thrown what the BBC had known up on its head. "We were losing ground fast, and needed to figure out how to reconnect to our audience and—quite frankly—our staff," Younge wrote in an email exchange with Deborah.[1]

Around the BBC, you could feel lower staff morale in the air, in no small part because the BBC's historic ability to produce its own programs was under threat. Through government mandate, the BBC's in-house production team was always guaranteed the right to produce 50 percent of BBC programs. The remaining programs were up for competition between privately owned independent producers, who were guaranteed 25 percent, with the final 25 percent being a creative competition between the in-house production team and independent producers outside the BBC. Over time, the independent producers were winning a clear majority of the competitions, and they were now demanding that the in-house guaranteed programming should be reduced or abolished. For Younge, this would be a massive strategic loss for the BBC, not only in terms of reduced employment, but also in terms of the network's need to produce and own an intellectual property portfolio of content.

Younge called upon friends at the Enterprise Development Group in Silicon Valley to help find a solution. Together, they formulated a stimulus strategy by expanding and diversifying the program development funnel. Younge put in a crowdsourcing process for new show ideas, called, "iCreate—Ideas from Everyone. Everywhere." The aim was to leverage the scale of the in-house studio by engaging the maximum number of people in the process of generating and iterating ideas. The platform was launched as part of a major staff engagement effort, attended by over a thousand employees in meetings across the country, putting iCreate into the context of business-critical needs and digital disruption.

One show, titled *Mr. Mum,* was submitted by Chris McMally, a BBC health and safety officer whose day job was ensuring that staff in the office and on location were working within legal safety parameters. McMally was riding his bike one day and a show idea about a single dad with two kids and no domestic skills came to him, and now he saw an opportunity to submit the idea on iCreate. Other BBC staff weighed in on *Mr. Mum* through likes and comments, yet McMally's show needed some structure and a comedic touch. Anne McNaught, a learning producer three hundred miles away in BBC Scotland, suggested McMally take a look at a book she had read called *How to Get Things Really Flat: A Male Approach to Ironing.*[2] Then, the BBC comedy department stepped in, seeing the comedic potential of combining McMally's story world and McNaught's male pseudoscience. They brought in Chris and Anne and introduced them to a comedy producer and writer, and together they went on to create a script.

iCreate also resulted in a broadcast film called *Make My Dream,* after Matt Walker, a BBC learning editor in Bristol, and

Neil Churchill, from the political unit in Millbank, separately posed ideas about a wish-fulfillment type show. "Until BBC iCreate came along, there was no outlet for ideas for those who didn't already work in TV production," Churchill said. "BBC iCreate helped me focus my idea into something more tangible and targeted. It gives me immense satisfaction to know that I can now contribute creative ideas to the BBC that are outside my day job," he continued. Walker added that he felt they were part of a "really collaborative process with access to people who could make your ideas happen," according to an internal BBC document.

In its first six months of existence, iCreate had more than 1,900 active users, and anyone could submit a show idea based on a specific direction or an open call for ideas. Users could improve show ideas, and, according to Alisa Orr, head of BBC Production's innovation unit, "[iCreate] proves that creativity exists right across the BBC, just waiting to be unlocked." One staff-engagement session ended with a female employee in tears. When asked what was wrong, she said, "I've worked here twenty-five years and no one has ever asked me for my ideas. Ever."[3]

So, what did iCreate do for the BBC? It included:

- an idea system in which anyone in the entire company can participate;

- a process to grow and incubate new ideas;

- standardization in ways to develop a blueprint;

- a collaboration between employees in disparate parts of the company who generally would not cross paths or interact.

What made iCreate so successful is that the process allowed anyone in any corner of the company to participate in an idea platform, thus democratizing the process and the value that each person could bring to the organization.

Improvisational Innovation

In her book, *The Risk Factor: Why Every Organization Needs Big Bets, Bold Characters, and the Occasional Spectacular Failure*,[4] Deborah introduced a new innovation methodology, and we believe in it so strongly that we brought it back in this chapter to highlight the process needed for the People Equation. Improvisational Innovation solves the problem for the senior executive who ponders the questions, "What do my people know that could be valuable to our business?" "How do I encourage them to give me their best ideas, and how do I most effectively test and implement them?"

Improvisational Innovation shows leaders how to build a system to encourage, stimulate, foster, capture, test, and implement these good ideas, whether they are improvements to the company's products, services, or a measure for cost-savings on infrastructure.

From the employee perspective, do they even know what to do if they have a great idea? Who do they turn to? Is there an "idea system" in place? If an innovative culture is nonexistent, or a lack of trust exists throughout the organization, does the employee take the risk to share his or her idea with their own manager, who might squash what could be a potentially good idea? Or—perhaps worse—does the manager who sees the value in the idea opt to take credit for it himself? Does the organization offer an incentive to those who want to share a good idea? These are some of the questions that get resolved by implementing a structured Improvisational Innovation process like the one carefully outlined below. The result of practicing Improvisational Innovation is an organization that can sustainably and significantly grow its top line, while retaining, encouraging, and exciting its most valuable employees.

The methodology behind Improvisational Innovation can work for any organization because it is an accessible and actionable approach to building on the assets a company currently has—

driving small, incremental steps while also increasing the likelihood of a major breakthrough. It focuses on accelerating ideas that advance the company and builds a culture that is fast and adaptive without interrupting the bottom line. Because this type of innovation encourages entrepreneurship (even "intrapreneurship") and the freedom to experiment in creative pursuits, it just might keep a company's greatest talent from jumping ship. If an organization can make space for an entrepreneurial-type employee to access the resources and rewards of a big company, chances are the organization will have less of an attrition issue and simultaneously position itself for growth.

Tackling the Unconscious Bias

In the context of the People Equation, Improvisational Innovation has the potential to tackle the unconscious bias, and here's why. As human beings, we can't help but to place judgment. From the moment someone walks into a room, we size them up for what we believe they can and cannot do. Based on someone's age, level of experience, education, gender, prior work history, the dialect of their voice, paycheck, and so on, we determine their capability and value. But the reality is that we need to look past the superficial and what's documented on paper and thoroughly understand the broad talents that each person brings to the table—how they spend time in and outside the office.

What we advocate for in the Improvisational Innovation process is an initial blind submission of anyone's idea. As explained in more detail below, a small vetting group decides which ideas move forward in the innovation process, but initially even this group is unaware of the identify of the inventor. We have found time and time again through a blind submission process that managers have no idea about the vast talents of their employees. They have described this process as "baffling" or being "pleasantly surprised." Some say, "I had no idea that this person had

Five Factors behind the Methodology of Improvisational Innovation

1. Democratize (allowing anyone to participate) the ideation platform so that great ideas can bubble up from anyone any time.

Inventors (innovators) are currently defined and determined by the industry they are in and curtail anyone else from participating. In Big Pharma, for example, where innovation is market driven, scientists become the innovators. In software or SaaS (software-as-a-service), it's the engineering team. In fashion, it is designers, and so on. In the innovation capital of the world, Silicon Valley, there is an adopted belief that every person is responsible for the success or failure of an organization. If other organizations adopted this same mindset, it would allow for broader participation in the invention process. The powerful difference in Improvisational Innovation is that inspiration can come from everyone, in any role, in every corner of the company. However, to effectively democratize the ideation process, there has to be a standard of acceptance when someone shares an idea, and an environment of optimism must exist so that anyone feels encouraged to propel their idea forward.

2. Adopt a formal process that will enable execution on a specific timeline.

The inventor's idea needs to move from concept to prototype and beyond, with a complete understanding from all involved of what to do and how long it will take. A formal process allows time for experimentation, additional staff support, market research, financial investment, and accelerated implementation. This process adheres to a specific schedule that everyone is aware of and which will enable an idea to seamlessly move from ideation to execution. The process will work best if a company adopts a technology "sandbox" component (SaaS or cloud based) to monitor, gate-keep and foster collaborative experimentation, and apply the appropriate business models.

3. Ensure that the inventor has access to the right people at the right time.

A great idea needs an advocate who can strengthen the idea, shepherd it throughout the organization, get it to the right people at the right time, and be on the hunt for a business unit to potentially fund and prototype it. Additionally, the inventor should network with colleagues outside the business unit they work in, and even be in position to become part of the business unit where the invention best fits. For example, if an idea comes from a financial analyst (who is a robotics hobbyist), but the idea is positioned for a robotics system unit, the inventor should have the opportunity to network and do a temporary work detail in that unit so that he or she gains a deeper understanding of how that unit operates and how the invention best fits in. This will ensure that all viable ideas on the table are not left unattended.

4. Reward the inventor.

If someone has brought you a bold bet that results in significant revenue increase or cost savings, organizational leadership needs to recognize the inventor and his or her team and reward them. The inventor should receive special recognition, be known for the product they invented, and have equity and ownership in the product comparable to what a founder's equity share would be outside the corporation.

5. Archive all ideas, good and not so good.

Ideas not viable today might just be perfect in the future. Lyn Heward, the former president and chief operating officer of Cirque du Soleil, described how the company warehouses failed or unused show concepts and acts, sometimes finding the perfect use for these ideas a decade later. It also catalogs unique talent in every corner of the globe and uses this database as an inspiration for future shows. To continue with its mission to "constantly evoke the imagination, invoke the senses and provoke the emotions of people around the world,"[5] Cirque du Soleil has developed some of the most advanced processes for continuing to enable groundbreaking innovation.

Reprinted with permission, from *The Risk Factor*

an interest in product development or the creativity they brought to an existing idea."

Allow your people to be their authentic selves, where they can freely submit ideas far beyond what they do day to day, and you will generate greater knowledge of their full and unanticipated talents and learn how to harness what they have to offer. You may discover that sometimes the greatest creativity comes from people you never thought had it.

Embrace Your Quirky People

By definition, creativity is "the ability to make new things or think of new ideas." Creativity must come from people who think about the world differently; otherwise, the ideas they come up with would have been dreamed up already and wouldn't be new and creative. Given that they think differently, these people are unlikely to conform to all our social norms—in other words, they may be quirky.

So why, if we value creativity, do we stifle our greatest creative, entrepreneurial types? Often, "the quirkies" just don't fit in. Perhaps they don't have the right business refinement or pedigree or look awkward on the golf course or in the office. Even more so, they tend to work differently. Perhaps they like to stand, have difficulty sitting, or pace. Isaac Asimov, the science fiction author and essayist, admits that isolation and unusual, embarrassing behavior play an integral role in his creativity, saying, "My feeling is that as far as creativity is concerned, isolation is required. The creative person is, in any case, continually working at it. His mind is shuffling his information at all times, even when he is not conscious of it. . . . The presence of others can only inhibit this process, since creation is embarrassing."[6]

One of my colleagues in Silicon Valley described to me a case in which a programmer asked to work on a project. The programmer was quirky in the extreme; he wouldn't look the project lead in the eye and spent most of his time staring intently at his own shoes. The brief interview, such as it was, revealed that the interviewee was unaware of how badly some of his inter-view responses came across. The interviewee talked at length about his video game play, while responses on work topics were monosyllabic. So the interviewer decided to hand him a small, difficult project—to work with an embedded computer—that he knew the interviewee was not familiar with. The interviewer asked him whether he could get some application code that they had been struggling with to function properly on this computer. The interviewee, without pausing, sat down, plugged the board in, and spent the next twelve hours glued to a screen. After twelve hours, he got up, handed the board to the interviewer, and said, "It's done."

The interviewer took the computer back to one of the members of the team that invented the application, who, in an exas-perated voice, said, "We've been trying to do that for a month and still haven't got it working!" The interviewee figured it out in twelve hours. The lesson here is to judge the output rather than the person/worker.

Until you embrace your quirky people and look beyond their surface failings, it's often difficult to grasp the true value they may provide. By embracing quirky people, we have the opportunity to think, act, and create differently, which will result in growth and innovation. This growth may begin in incremental changes, but before you know it, these small changes may lead to monumental changes once you establish trust and understanding of the value being brought to the table.

The People Equation Prescription

The Improvisational Innovation Process
TWELVE STEPS OVER NINE MONTHS

Improvisational Innovation is a bottom-up process that lends itself to engaging every employee in every corner of your company. The way we have designed the process at Vorto Consulting is as an annual twelve-step method executed over a nine-month period, with a three-month "off season." However, we have worked with some firms that prefer more rapid prototyping and have opted to design a biannual innovation process. By adopting a specific and consistent time line each year, the method sends the right message for creating an innovative culture and gets employees into the mindset of when and how their ideas will be heard and potentially executed upon and commercialized. We personally like to begin an innovation process in September because it correlates with going back to school and gives people summer downtime to further develop their ideas.

Improvisational Innovation should be led by a small team (five people or less) whose sole job is to oversee the process year after year. The Improvisational Innovation team provides expertise, training, a lending ear for a safe and trusted environment, connectivity to other parts of the organization, and is the place for an entrepreneurial type to turn to for all of his or her prototyping and entrepreneurial needs. This team can be housed in an existing department, such as human resources, or be independent. In the case of Qualcomm, where Deborah got to observe the company's ImpaQT program (the name of their bottom-up innovation process), the company has a workforce of thirty-three thousand people worldwide, but only a small team of five lead the ImpaQT program for the entire company. The ImpaQT team's roles ranged from program manager, technology lead, and IT manager to marketing and partnerships manager, serving to meet most every need of the inventors.

PHASE I: IDEATION

Step I: Announce the Program

Before beginning this type of program, senior management in the company must frankly assess where they are and where the world is going. This is where the leadership team can gather and put skin in the game, providing the message of commitment from the top. The Improvisational Innovation process is announced to the organization and invites participation around specific cross-cutting themes (preferably three to five) that cover the whole business of the organization and focus on opportunity spaces, underaddressed needs, or pain points. An example of cross-cutting themes are the Internet of Everything, Data Demand, and one category that is more general and addresses the future five to ten years out, such as Blue Sky. An all-employee meeting is arranged to discuss the logistics of how the process works, from idea submission to prototype.

Step 2: Submit the Idea

The Improvisational Innovation team sets a deadline for idea submissions, giving employees time to vet and improve upon their idea in addition to seeking out possible colleagues who may be inclined to work on the project. Ideas are submitted anonymously to the Improvisational Innovation management team through an internal database that collects the following information:

- Idea title
- Idea description
- Cross-cutting theme category
- What is the opportunity?
- What is the problem you are trying to solve?
- How will the idea benefit the organization?

The idea submitters, from this point forward, are now referred to as *inventors*. Ideas are vetted by the Improvisational

Innovation management team strictly on merit (irrespective of an inventor's level, pay grade, education, or expertise) and narrowed down over the next few weeks. Idea submissions could number in the hundreds, depending on the size of the organization, but they will likely be narrowed down to a handful. Ideas that do not pass the idea-submission phase are given feedback from an Improvisational Innovation management team member as to what could be improved for resubmission in a subsequent year.

For the ideas that move on, the inventor is now revealed to the management team and begins the next phase of the Improvisational Innovation process. Throughout the progression of the process—irrespective of how long an inventor is engaged in continuing with their idea—the inventor will be able to rely on the Improvisational Innovation team for advice, resources, and networking throughout the organization. As explained below, each inventor will be given time and be allocated a team of up to four people and a small amount of financial and in-kind resources. They will, however, be responsible to carry on their existing day job. Because of this additional responsibility, we have witnessed that throughout the process, a handful of inventors drop out for a variety of reasons, such as the project becomes too overwhelming (on top of their day job), they don't have a strong, commited team, or the inventor is not comfortable taking on an entrepreneurial pursuit. You will want to reinforce that, whatever the outcome, the inventor is learning how to become an entrepreneur using the company's time, money, and expertise—a golden opportunity for someone to develop new skills. We try to think of the opportunity as obtaining an advanced degree, such as an MBA, without having to pay for it.

PHASE II: PRODUCT DEVELOPMENT

Step 3: Appoint a Mentor

The inventor is appointed a mentor from the business unit in which the idea best fits. For example, if the inventor is an accountant but his or her idea fits into the robotics division of the company, the inventor will now be paired with a robotics expert from a product development standpoint. The mentor and mentee have two weeks to strengthen the idea and develop a written plan for proof of concept.

At a later time, if the idea continues to move through the Improvisational Innovation process, the inventor will be assigned an entrepreneurial/business mentor to start exploring the idea from product development, branding, marketing, and sales perspectives, beginning to place the idea within the context of the company's current or future operations.

Step 4: Create a 360 Steering Committee

A 360 steering committee is put in place for business leads to start to vet the idea from a company perspective. The committee consists of one member from each division that must contribute to the success of the idea, such as, but not limited to, legal, product design, technology, marketing, branding, and sales. The committee meets regularly and is first tasked with vetting each inventor's proof of concept. They then green-light the idea to the next level of the process. Once the proof of concept is approved, the committee identifies all the functions and activities that need to be addressed to propel the idea forward. Inventors' ideas that get approved to move on at this stage are given feedback from the steering committee.

Step 5: Protect Intellectual Property

Any and all intellectual property (IP)—patents, trademarks, copyrights, and trade secrets—that needs to be filed should be done by the company's general counsel/legal team at this stage. The inventor will work with the legal team on language that most comprehensively protects the idea, the inventor, and the company. This is a guarantee for inventors and the organization that the hard work, time, and funds invested in the creation of something new will be rewarded if the product or technology finds a market. The intangible asset of the IP is recognized as a valuable asset in that the invention can now be licensed, bought, or sold.

Step 6: Build a Team

The inventor has an opportunity to build a team of four internal employees, who add greatly to the success of the invention and must be willing to work above and beyond their daily job. The team should have all the expertise and complementary knowledge and skills to launch. They should be granted 20 percent time (one day per week) over a term of three months to prototype a product or new line of business. The team is granted a small budget (up to $3,000, for example) for the costs of the materials and components for the prototype. During this time, the inventor learns how to build a team that shares like-minded values and goals and how the chemistry of the team is critical to the invention's success. It is the role of the Improvisational Innovation management team to either educate the inventor on team success or bring in external experts who can teach the inventor the value and know-how of building a great team—because the team can make or break the invention.

As mentioned earlier, each member still has to conduct his or her daily job and accepts that additional hours (after hours, weekends, holidays) will be necessary to do both their day job and work on the inventor's prototype. In the event that the inventor is unable to assemble a team, the Improvisational Innovation management team will work with talent-development personnel to recommend people to work on the project team.

Step 7: Define Time Lines and Milestones

The inventor is assigned and meets regularly with an entrepreneurial/business mentor who can help lay out all the necessary deliverables and milestones that would go into a product launch. At this stage, there are likely to be many unknowns that will determine the success of the business, and, in line with Lean methods, the entrepreneur and mentor should design a plan that enables those unknowns to be resolved. For example, questions will arise about whether customers will accept the new product or service, so the plan may include a learning cycle in which a prototype product is released in a test market to validate the acceptability of the proposed solution. As another example, there may be a critical technical feature that needs to be proved to work. At this stage, time lines and milestones are there to identify the unknowns and to think of them in terms of provable hypotheses that can be tested with a Lean learning cycle.

Be prepared to utilize all the tools in a rapid prototyping tool kit, as well as going into test markets with the minimum product that is viable for that market. This well-worn route is the way in which you can understand the merit of your idea. But more than all this, plan time to reflect and understand what the results of those experiments mean. Well-designed learning cycles should influence your thinking about your product, its placement, and the market. Thinking of the lowest cost "experiment" that is needed to find the truth behind the unknowns, and then designing the plan around those experiments, will provide the entrepreneur with the most likely route to success.

Step 8: Organize a Networking/Talent Swap

The Improvisational Innovation teams helps the inventor network with the division where the idea best fits and helps facilitate either a full- or part-time talent swap in that division over the course of the project. In the example mentioned earlier, if an inventor is an accountant by day but a robotics hobbyist on the weekends and has a strong idea that has the potential to benefit the company, he or she deserves the time to sit in the robotics division for a given period of time. The talent swap is effective because it is a great way to help strengthen the invention, and it also helps retain employees perceived as having high potential.

PHASE III: LEARNING HOW TO BECOME AN ENTREPRENEUR AND SETTING THE BUSINESS MODEL

Step 9: Provide Entrepreneurial Training

Inventors may be brilliant in their area of expertise or passion, but they know very little about how to build a successful entrepreneurial venture. The Improvisational Innovation team now arranges for the inventor to begin to participate in entrepreneurial boot camps where the inventors learn the operational side of business, including, but not limited to, creating financial documents (income statements, balance sheets, and so on), sales forecasting, and gross and standard margins. Additional experts are also brought into the company to teach design thinking or to go deeper into Lean methods that might help in the inventor's prototype design and delivery process. It is at this stage that the inventor fully engages with the entrepreneurial mentor so that he or she is thinking about the comprehensive approach to rolling out the launch of the invention.

Step 10: Develop Strategic Partnerships

The inventor reconnects with the 360 steering committee to start seeking out potential internal and external partners from whom the invention would likely receive interest. It is the role of the committee to work with the inventor and respective mentors (product development and business mentors) to help shepherd and showcase the invention to divisions in the company and to potential outside partners, all leading up to striking early interest in the invention prior to Demo Day.

Step 11: Hold Prototype Demo Day

The goal of the Prototype Demo Day is to find sponsors to bid on the ideas and spin them forward into a particular business unit. Demo Day looks like a typical high-school science fair, where business leads cruise from booth to booth examining each prototype and vet whether they potentially fit into their business unit.

The inventor and his or her team offer their best elevator pitch for their product and say why they believe it should be adopted into a particular business unit within the company. The business lead should walk away hungry to have the invention in his or her division or at least want to continue the conversation. While on-site or shortly thereafter, the business leads fill out a questionnaire on each prototype, responding to questions such as:

- How do you rate this idea?

- Would you be interested in becoming a sponsor (adopting and absorbing the invention into your business unit)?

- If you are not interested in the invention, please share why.

- How would you improve this prototype?

Shortly after Demo Day, the Improvisational Innovation management team announces those inventions that will be adopted by a business unit, the P&L in support of the invention, and a time line/plan of when the invention will be on track to be commercialized. If a sponsor of a particular business unit does not adopt an invention, the invention stays in the Improvisational Innovation program and continues to be developed or gets parked with the ideas held in a database of unused projects. A venture capital fund set up by the company might offer to provide additional funding, and the invention can be commercialized by the Improvisational Innovation program should the invention not find a home internally within a division.

Step 12: Reward the Inventor

For those inventors whose ideas have been adopted into a business division, the inventor now decides whether he or she wants to stay in their existing job or move forward commercializing the invention. If the inventor wants to carry through, the inventor works with the sponsoring business lead on a plan, and additional talent and a budget are set for commercializing the invention. As mentioned earlier, the company will reward the inventor with equity in the invention, and the inventor's team will receive both monetary and recognition rewards for their participation.

WHAT HAPPENS NEXT

The result of the Improvisational Innovation process should be a new set of portfolio businesses with individuals who are now your rising stars. What happens now? You let each inventor choose whether he or she wants to stick to their current job or continue to build their invention to commercialization. Should an inventor want to stay in their current role, there are four other team members to tap who could help lead the invention in the adopted business unit.

Repeating the Improvisational Innovation process each year should offer the prospect that employees can turn into stakeholders and thus engage more deeply with the company and develop something that will be of tremendous value for it. Improvisational Innovation provides an environment for people to have the freedom to experiment, democratizes innovation participation rates, and, in its course, recognizes and rewards those individuals who bring new ideas to the organization. The process positions companies to embrace innovation and enables the company to evolve into the next generation. Just as the annual growth of a farmer's harvest depends on planting new crops each year, so too does a company depend on the continued cultivation of new businesses.

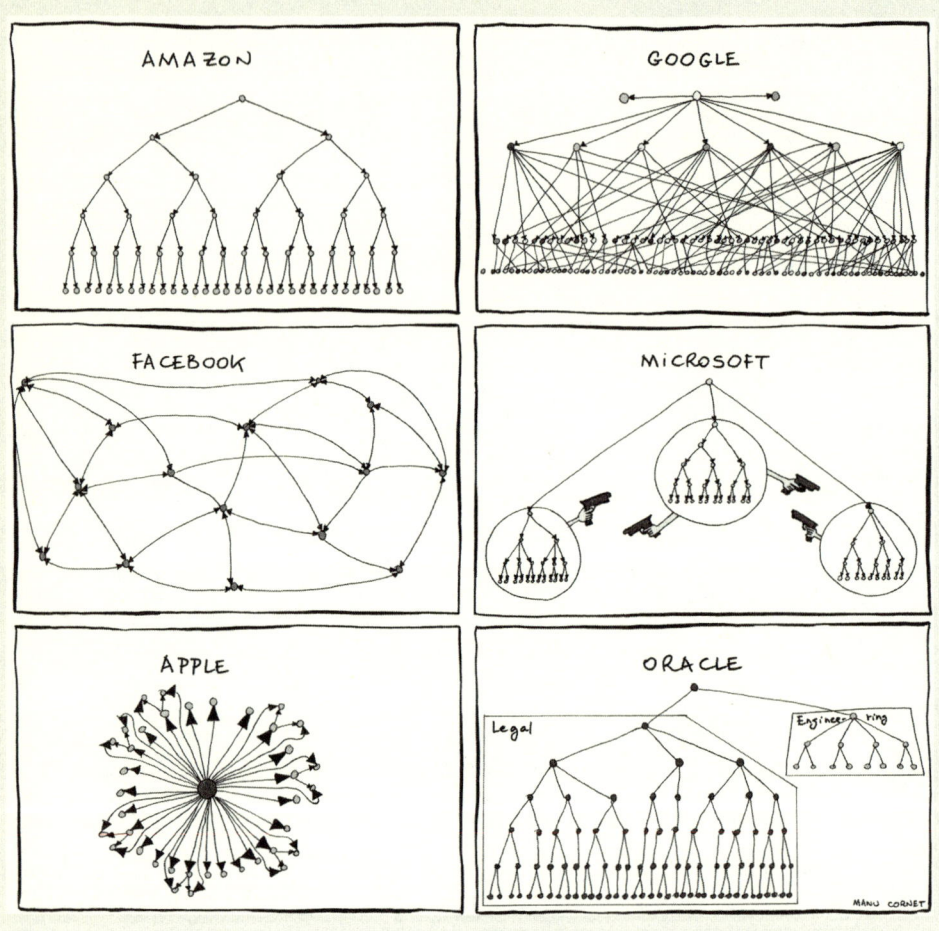

Hierarchy at work

What does your hierarchy look like?

CHAPTER 3

THE INVERTED ORGANIZATION

S am Metcalf has the calm demeanor of a missionary and the zeal of an evangelist. He is the CEO of a global organization known as CRM, a social entrepreneurship nonprofit that started in the United States but has now established partner organizations in twelve countries with operations in ninety-four countries. This group works overseas to establish local leaders and affiliate organizations that provide local finance to meet CRM's humanitarian and religious mission, which is executed by those same local groups. They are in some ways an enterprise planting organization.

While CRM does have religious-missionary origins, what is perhaps most interesting is how it started and how it is structured. It was founded in 1980, and all of its cofounders had been working at a traditional humanitarian-mission organization that inevitably became very hierarchical. These were people who had volunteered to help others because of the strength of their beliefs. They hadn't signed up to be controlled by a hierarchy. They had agreed to work in the nonprofit sector not because of the pay or glory, but because they had a vision for helping others, and autonomy was required to meet that vision. Together with a group of others, all in their twenties and thirties, these altruistic individuals wanted to experiment with novel ways of doing their work, but they found themselves in large, hierarchical organizations that weren't receptive to their ideas.

Metcalf and a small group of colleagues left their respective non-profits and established CRM, which has proved to be an experiment in devolving power away from a central leadership and bringing it to the foot soldiers doing the life-altering work. Now CRM has a staff of more than 530 people engaged in hard-to-reach places around the world, where each office is set up, supported, and run with the goal of creating an independent, self-sustaining entity. Once an overseas unit develops sound and independent leadership, the US organization relinquishes control. The only formal relationship is known as a "conext partnership," which is an agreement to work together with an explicitly relational, not organizational interaction. As Mr. Metcalf puts it, "I have no legal control, no organizational control, I have some influence."[1]

So how does CRM operate as a coherent group? Their agreement to work together includes a commitment to work according to a shared set of beliefs, values, mission, and vision. This is a written agreement between CRM and each office.

They are also careful about screening the people whom they admit to the organization, to ensure that the people share the same concept on three important factors—the "what, who and where," says Metcalf. For example, a prospective employee may go through a grueling exercise of assessing alignment. As Metcalf states it: "Is this what you want to do and does the organization want to do the same thing? Is that what you want to give your life to? What do you anticipate to be the outcomes?" The *who* is something such as "Are these the people you want to fight with, love with, perhaps have the privilege of dying with?" The *where* is the place that you want to go. To play a ball game, you better know "the game, the team and the ballpark," as Metcalf puts it.

The people in the organization have diverse backgrounds, but the result of this careful screening is an organization that is bound together with people who reveal a closely aligned worldview. They also share a deep commitment to the organization and the work they are engaged in. Not only do CRM staff members probe each individual deeply to understand his or her underlying motivations, they also test them. Each person they put overseas has to raise funds; those who don't have the entrepreneurial wherewithal to do this, self-select out. To come to alignment on the what, who, and where, as well as to raise funds, is a process that takes, on average, two years. Yet despite the hurdles to get in, CRM has no formal recruiting organization. They don't actively seek out candidates for these challenging roles; the candidates find them. "It happens through word of mouth," says Metcalf.

The management, however, is anything but loose. The local organizations have supervisory boards to provide accountability. Each national organization gathers and reports metrics. "Our staff turn in metrics yearly, names and numbers—quality and results can all be quantified" says Metcalf. However, the independent nature of the organization yields a few surprising facets. "The kicker is that I can't force them [to turn in their metrics]." The metrics create a common sense of what good performance looks like—more like a benchmarking exercise than tool of management control. When there are performance problems, the organization reacts, but it is not the CEO who is doing the firing. "There are some that will hit the eject button and say 'we are out,'" explains Metcalf. In other situations, Metcalf, who is CEO of the US mother organization, may initiate a conversation with local leadership—when, for example, the person leading the organization in a country is not the right choice. But Metcalf is quick to point out, "I can't force it."

In addition to the shared beliefs, values, mission, and vision, the organization has regular conferences to engage in strategic planning, but they also have a much more important role in keeping people aligned with one another and with the overall mission of the organization. "Trust and emotional connection is key," according to Metcalf. Through these conferences, personal relationships are built, and as such, "We have no trouble sharing people and resources across regions," according to Metcalf.

The conferences enable best practices to be shared because

there are "tools and processes" that the organization seeks to deploy in different regions. However, as Metcalf mentions, "What we are doing has to be contextualized. What we are doing in Washington isn't going to work in Central China."

One of the staffers at CRM remarked, "In our organization, when something is successful, other people want to replicate it" and "that allows for rapid innovation." As a not-for-profit organization, CRM views its role as to "take new ground, and go where other people can't go, or don't want to go," says Metcalf. This propensity to take on new challenges means that they are confronted with something different each time, and this theme of constant change and innovation is something that runs throughout the organization. As Metcalf puts it: "We tell our people that change is constant here; if you don't like change, you are with the wrong outfit."

CRM shows a model for dealing with constant change by creating:

- a high-trust, low-control environment;

- ample opportunity both to compare relative performance and share best practices;

- the ability to bind people together with a vigorous set of beliefs, values, mission, and vision;

- opportunities to create emotional connections with the organization;

- processes that restrict admission to those who are deeply aligned with the organization.

Firms That Build Other Firms: The Silicon Valley Model

From our point of view, CRM reminds us that one of the key ingredients of Silicon Valley's success is, no doubt, "the firm that builds other firms"—the venture capitalist (VC) model. In 1978, the first year that modern technology-oriented VC firms could have a successful fund-raising effort after the oil crash in 1973, VC firms raised $750 million, considered a high-water mark at the time.

Initially, these VC firms were founded to do the type of investing that private equity companies could not easily do and were a world away from the activity of the corporate investors. The modern VC, however, provides much more than just cash to nurture a growing enterprise. For example, Sequoia Capital, the famed venture capital firm located in Silicon Valley, has a department dedicated to finding and hiring people for their portfolio companies. Most Silicon Valley VCs give ample advice to their (sometimes young) founders as to how to go about the process of building their businesses. There are even specialist VC firms, such as Tech-Rx, that, for example, work on engaging deeply with early-stage companies to correct performance problems or sort out deep, viability-scale problems. Consider how the interaction between a VC firm and a founder differs from the interaction between a typical hierarchical company and the senior manager of a department in it. The hierarchical organization will typically expect:

- the department manager to serve the needs of the corporation;

- to control, often precisely, the activities of the department manager;

- to reward compliance with company desires with promotion.

VCs flourish because they do things that traditional Taylorist companies do not and align themselves with the needs of a fluid economy. Typically, they will expect:

- to provide the founder with things that he/she requires, especially ample capital;

- the founder to control activities in his/her start-up so that
  the VC doesn't have to worry about it;

- to amply reward the success of the founder with substantial equity in the company and financial returns that will
  be many times annual salary in a good exit. Compliance
  with the VC has limited meaning unless it leads to company success.

The orientation of the VC is completely different from the normal manager in a hierarchical company. The hierarchical company will expect a department manager to serve the needs of the
corporation, whereas the VC is there to serve the needs of the
start-up. Growth of VC funding has been fueled by expanding
opportunities for it, which is fueled by the willingness of entrepreneurs to start new businesses, which has been fueled by the
potential rewards that are available to them if they do.

In essence, the normal organization structure has been turned
on its head. VCs essentially provide for the needs of the entrepreneur, and in doing so have driven their own success. This is what
we mean by the *inverted organization*—an organization that is oriented around the needs of its people and making them successful rather than around the needs and desires of the most senior
person. It's important to realize that in almost all enterprises,
customers buy what people on the front line produce. Customers don't consume the decisions and management directives of
the CEO or any other full-time manager. As such, the role of the
manager has to be to support the needs of the front line, not the
other way around.

VC firms are typically the funders in a network of companies
that operate as a people-centric enterprise. In addition, VCs build
relationships with service providers, other investors, and strategic partners, all with the potential to make you wildly successful
over an accelerated time period. Connect with the right VC, as
Mark Zuckerberg did with Peter Thiel, and you can go from zero

to stratospheric in a short amount of time. VCs and their relationships become cheerleading sideliners with you as the quarterback at the big game.

In Silicon Valley, this coaching, cheering, and support from the sidelines leads to the development of a cadre of entrepreneurs who have led successful businesses, and then it tends to have a trickle-down effect. For many VC firms, the very entrepreneurs they fund later become the angel investors and advisors of the next generation of start-ups. The trickling down is what keeps Silicon Valley's prowess going and growing.

In the People Equation and a fluid economy, if you don't actively devolve power to individuals, you erode the capacity to develop new leadership talent. Large corporations have tried to get into the act and have frequently set up their own internal venture arms. In so doing, they will have to create conditions around their innovators to help them and motivate them to achieve success. A devolved organization structure will be critical here, as the attempt to control people is, as we have seen, loaded with either explicit or implicit notions of threat, causing at best disengagement and at worst the active pursuit of a poor idea that was created while bypassing the cerebrum.

A Technology Firm That Creates Other Firms

The model of a company that creates other companies is not unique to venture capital. In Cambridge, England, there is a cluster of companies that bill themselves as "consultancies" but frequently are companies that create other ventures. One of these consultancies is The Technology Partnership (TTP), where Dr. Sam Hyde serves as the firm's cerebral, soft-spoken managing director.

TTP has a dual business model. Their bread and butter is to work on tough technical problems for clients across the globe, be it designing a specialty print head or inventing ingenious drug-delivery hardware. Drug companies, for example, don't have the expertise in hardware or microfluidics that some drug-delivery systems require, and TTP provides this expertise. The other element of their business model is to incubate technology ventures internally, often for years, before spinning them out as an independent entity.

They've been successfully developing highly innovative technical solutions for almost thirty years. What are the secrets of TTP's success? We have identified five key factors that help them run a successful inverted organization:

- Rigorously nonhierarchical

- Focused on hiring well

- Uses intrinsic motivators rather than a typical carrot-and-stick approach

- Creates alignment without formality

- Offers a benign and supportive environment

Rigorously nonhierarchical. Dr. Hyde is himself unusual within TTP in that he is one of only seven people in the three-hundred-person-strong organization who actually has a management title, although he is quick to point out that even that fact is deemphasized. While there are a small number of functional people in HR and finance, the overwhelming majority of people, some 250, are consultants who form ad hoc teams that deliver technical expertise for clients. Within those teams are team leaders; however, that role can switch from one project to the next, and in principle any consultant can be a team leader. The pool of consultants is also the same group that develops the business and brings in work as well as the frontline people who actually go into the lab to develop the highly technical solutions that TTP is known for. There is no formality as to who does business development, leads teams, and does frontline technical work, and it is usual that people move back and forth between these roles in the course of their careers. The only management titles are the leads of the six groups that form the consulting company, each consisting of thirty to fifty people, and the managing director, Dr. Hyde.

Focused on hiring well. "It's about hiring well," according to Hyde.[2] Like many other companies that have successful inverted organizations, there is a focus on getting the right type of highly committed people into the organization in the first place. One PhD holder from Cambridge University said, "Every science PhD in the University of Cambridge that wants to be on the technical side of technical products would love to work at The Technology Partnership." It has a towering reputation as a great place to work, but also, more than that, as a tough place to get into. Stories abound from recent University of Cambridge PhDs about long and demanding technical interviews, where candidates answer questions about everything from fluidics to optics, often for several hours. The interviews are not just technical, the interviewers also work to get to know the person and what makes them tick. The interview process is so tough that few University of Cambridge PhDs, even those who are universally described as technically excellent, make it through the interview process. Hyde freely admits, "Sometimes we make mistakes in turning away good candidates."

For TTP, they look for people who are very good technically but who more importantly have the ability to look across a range of technical and business issues so that they can understand the commercial potential of any technical idea. Like many of the other inverted organizations we looked at, TTP also looks for high levels of intrinsic motivation: "They need to have an intrinsic interest," says Hyde. "They need to have a passion for commercialization." TTP also makes sure to hire a wide variety of technical talent. "Diversity is pretty key for us," says Hyde. According to Hyde, idea generation is really about the context and exposure to many different fields; the cross-fertilization of needs, technology, and business; and business models, so the firm seeks people from a range of technical backgrounds to create that trait internally. This is also reflected within the company. It is notable that in discussions with frontline employees, they are able, with pride, to articulate their area of technical specialization as well as the specialization of those around them. Hyde also admits that having a high bar for hiring has its downsides. "It limits our headcount growth." But they view maintaining high standards within the firm as more important than growing explosively.

Uses intrinsic motivators rather than a typical carrot-and-stick approach. Rather than traditional performance management, TPP motivates by providing autonomy, encouraging mastery, and developing purpose. These management concepts, first promulgated by Daniel Pink, are practiced at TTP. According to Gallup, only 33 percent of the American workforce and 13 percent of the global workforce is engaged in their work.[3] Yet performance management through metrics and targets is an almost universal aspect of the modern corporate existence. TTP has understood that metrics and targets often create disengagement, precisely because they are a mechanism of control. So why would your most individualistic and inventive people, the very people required for success in the fluid economy, want to engage with and be controlled by that type of a system? Furthermore, traditional carrot-and-stick motivators have the tendency to create focus and thus reduce the type of lateral thinking that work in the fluid economy requires. As such, TTP takes entirely the reverse approach—as an inverted organization, it promotes high levels of autonomy. As Hyde says, "We trust them to understand that as a business we have to make money—but you can judge how to use your time and pursue your real interests."

Frontline autonomy and empowerment are not merely something articulated at the top of the organization. Frontline technical employees noted that, "You fill out your timesheet, but after that you are expected to just get on with the job."

The notion of mastery is also considered important at TTP. The idea that individuals have their own particular talent and capability that they bring to the organization, and that they should spend time working in their area of expertise while continuing to grow more broadly, is one of the ways in which TTP motivates its people. Developing purpose is also clear at TTP. The projects they undertake are for clients with clear and pressing business purposes, and this is injected into the organization.

Create alignment without formality. Perhaps one of the most surprising things about The Technology Partnership is how aligned people are across the organization. In our interviews, operational consultants seemed to articulate the same principles of success, sometimes almost word for word, as the managing director. Yet this level of alignment happens with shockingly little formality.

"We don't write any of it down, because if you write it down it becomes dogma," says Hyde. "We have norms not rules, because norms can be challenged." He goes on, "People are told they have the right to think differently. People feel free to challenge a norm." These norms are communicated through frequent informal interactions. "Working at TTP requires a social personality," Hyde says. "Some engineers can be a little introverted—but that doesn't work for us." In addition to social communication of these norms, as in many other inverted organizations that we studied, more deliberate attempts to discuss aspects of the business occur through frequent off-site meetings. For TTP, these are typically chaired conversations with a particular focus. People start to be invited to these meetings after working with TTP for a few months. According to Hyde, this does two things. First, it helps develop the people who are invited. "When you ask them to come, they think really hard about the topic." It also enables the ideas to be developed. Hyde is quick to note that the lack of proceduralization may not necessarily be the fastest method—"We accept a certain level of inefficiency"—but it enables flexibility in the system and is more motivating than large tomes of process books that people are required to follow. At the end of the day, "It's about what is inside people's heads."

Offer a benign and supportive environment. The management, such as it exists in TTP, is deliberately benign and supportive. The notion that talented individuals get to pursue their own passions within the context of a moneymaking business is at the core of how TTP operates. The natural result of this is that individuals in the corporation develop ideas, some of which are suited for exploitation outside the principal consulting model. There are a variety of different destinations for these businesses: some are developed within the TTP umbrella outside the consulting groups, many result in trade sales, and there is precedent for an IPO. The single theme for all these businesses is that they are technology focused. How the business is developed is clearly dependent on the nature of that technology, what it takes to bring the business to market, and what the team needs. It seems almost that the way in which this company generates other companies springs out of its desire to have a people-centric organization.

The willingness of TTP to spin parts of the organization out, the tendency to keep the organization small rather than allow hierarchy to slip in, and the relentless focus on the people in the organization all make it obvious that TTP is the antithesis of the empire-building mentality that possesses many Taylorist organizations. In short, TTP is successful because it isn't trying to control its people and has tried to create an environment that is optimal for smart, inventive people. In so doing, TTP has succeeded in an ideas business.

In many ways, TTP is at the vanguard of the fluid economy. They are entirely focused on delivering commercially viable technical solutions. They have also provided a model for how an inverted organization might function.

The People Equation Prescription

So how do you invert your organization? How do you go from a world where the frontline employee serves the corporation to one where the corporation serves the need of the frontline employee? There are two methods: grow the inverted part of the organization, or reform the part of the organization that isn't inverted.

GROW THE INVERTED ORGANIZATION

Nothing grows in the shadow of a tall tree, so control by and proximity to the mother organization will merely strangle the new enterprise. For an inverted organization to be successful, it must allow the new enterprise to grow up without being crowded out by the thorns of the originating entity. As we observe from the case examples of CRM, VC firms, and TTP, these are organizations that plant other organizations. In these cases, the planting organization deliberately seeks to develop the planted entity, cultivate it, and grow it to stand on its own, and then they relinquish control. To invert an organization will require developing it to do just that. In chapter 2 we talked about the Improvisational Innovation process, which enables your organization to build independent entities. Running that process is a team that directs and cultivates the internal start-ups that the organization creates. It is the role of that team to build a culture of intrapreneurship and entrepreneurship and create the capability within the people of the organization to embrace those responsibilities. By delivering successful internal start-ups, which are allowed a high degree of autonomy over time, it will be possible to invert the organization around those businesses.

REFORM THE ORGANIZATION THAT IS NOT INVERTED

There are few industries that are more challenged in the post-Internet economy than brick-and-mortar booksellers. With competitive attacks from disruptive Internet-based booksellers such as Amazon, as well as electronic book delivery through e-readers such as the Nook and Kindle, traditional brick-and-mortar retail book outlets seemed like an anachronism, destined to go the way of the dodo or Blockbuster video stores. Waterstones, the largest chain bookstore in England, felt these pressures acutely. In 2011, they were £170 million ($260 million) in debt and losing money. However, after a remarkable turnaround in 2015, they are profitable—and more than merely profitable; while chains like Barnes and Noble are shutting down stores to conserve cash, Waterstones is planning new store locations.

What was the source of this turnaround? It was a fundamental decision to respond to these monumental changes by making business decisions at the store level. Prior to Waterstones' turnaround, they, like many large book retailers, had centrally planned stores. Publishers would pay the bookstore for the choicest display areas, and each outlet in the chain would have to follow suit. A central office planogram ensured that the outlets prioritized the displays in the same way.

For Waterstones, that all changed when James Daunt took over as CEO. Many of the chain bookstore CEOs of that era were generic retail executives. Daunt, however, had started out in retail as an indie bookseller. As such, he had a healthy disdain for central control and bureaucratic processes, but most importantly he understood how a local store manager could better cater to the needs of his local clientele. At the time he took over, the company was broke and the promotional income from publishers was an important source of revenue. However, in a move that was considered suicidal by some, he decided to end the central control of store layouts and the promotional revenues that came with it. He handed layout decisions to the local store managers. More than this, he allowed local stores to make decisions about which books to discount and which to sell at full price and shrank the size of the head office. Suddenly, the store managers ceased to be the client of headquarters; instead, headquarters was the servant of the stores.

The result was that local managers were better able to cater to the needs of their local population. The store that was situated in a middle-class neighborhood wound up having a very different look and feel than stores that were in, say, the central business district. In one example, a store in downtown London, rather than devoting its storefront display to the latest best seller, had a display that promoted a classic as a great beach read. Freed from the requirement to promote particular books, stores held more titles in stock. And, because the stores more closely matched the tastes of the potential customers in their area, the number of books that had to be returned to the publishers dropped from 23 percent to an astonishing 4 percent. What is more, those that ran the stores were imbued with a sense of purpose, while they were busier and were working harder.

Daunt has been quoted as saying: "You love being in a shop where people are busy. It's much better than being out the back, filling up boxes of returns and thinking your life is a drudgery of doing pointless administrative tasks for some nameless bureaucracy of a head office who you *despise* because they just dump innumerable amounts of crap books on you."[4]

By creating an inverted organization, Waterstones has done what Internet retailers could not—provide a destination that appealed to the local population while simultaneously creating a better environment for those who worked there. They offered the consumer a local physical experience in a way that Amazon could not.

One of the major problems that exists in trying to reform an organization to be more focused on the individual is that the organization is filled with people who are used to being told what to do. While being in an organization that is oriented toward the needs of the most senior person may be frustrating and restrictive, that doesn't mean that people in that organization are

capable of operating in one that is different. One of the first challenges is developing in your people the capability to operate any
other way. People are likely to need problem-solving capacity
that doesn't exist, the discipline to deploy with consistent quality
without being watched, or a thousand and one other things that
are dependent on the capability of the people that you are seeking to develop. In the Waterstones transformation, half the managers left the company.

One method to develop your people comes from Toyota and
is known as *Hoshin Kanri*, which translates to "breakthrough
deployment" or "policy deployment." *Hoshin Kanri* is seen by
purists principally as a way to develop people in the organization
to be able to take on a particular theme or problem. In a *Hoshin
Kanri* process, you ask everyone in the organization to work on
the same themes, but in their own domain. *Hoshin Kanri* is closely
linked with what is known as a "catch ball" process. In this process, the top manager of an organization suggests a few organizational themes—for example, "cost" or "quality"—and it is up
to the people who report to that manager to develop an initiative
that matches that theme that will improve the capability of the
people in the organization. For example, if the senior leader was
to say "quality," those reporting to him might suggest improving
final output quality in, say, packaging the product. They would
assign people within the organization to address that problem
both to develop those individuals and to improve corporate performance in that area. Note that the senior leader doesn't exactly
tell those reporting to him what to do. That leader merely suggests a topic area and expects those reporting upward to come up
with the details. This practice over time develops the capacity of
the front line to identify and solve problems and think indepen-
dently. Over time, it means that the senior leader is becoming less
and less directive and more of a coach. It requires a deep commitment to the long-term development of your people.

OTHER MODELS

The model of a highly devolved organization has other precedents. Berkshire Hathaway, Warren Buffet's enormously successful, diversified conglomerate, is a highly devolved organization. Despite having more than 340,000 employees in its combined companies, the headquarters has only twenty-five people as staff. Warren Buffet himself repeatedly describes how the managers in Berkshire's portfolio companies know much more about their respective businesses than he does. He characterizes his chairmanship of these companies as "limited" and frequently eschews activism in the management of these companies. Yet Berkshire provides these very large enterprises with capital—and, of course, wisdom. In short, Berkshire eschews controlling a company in favor of providing them knowledge. Many of the examples of devolved or inverted organizations that emerge are high growth, successful, and flourishing.

Marvin Bower, the storied management consultant and the man who built McKinsey & Company to the size and reputation it has today, warned of the dangers of hierarchies. His only radio address touched on the pernicious dangers of this organizational structure. In 1966, he remarked, "I believe that leaders and leadership teams working together in a proper design will run the business more effectively than by hierarchical, command-and-control managing. But I can't prove that. And there are no models."[5]

Perhaps we can now say that he was right—that some of the companies that have emerged since 1966 with an inverted organizational model are not only still with us but thriving.

In the People Equation, managers should devolve their authority outward. In a part of their organization where innovation is most critical, this may mean seeking to empower devolved leadership to the point where they are successfully managing their own enterprise. That enterprise may be independent of the main organization. This level of devolution will not come naturally to the typical corporate manager, but it is critical to allow the corporation to survive in the fluid economic future before us. Nurturing and rewarding those who take the risks to lead those units is important. The rewards should be substantial both to reflect the success of those organizations and to maintain an attitude of shared value and trust.

Managers trying to respond to a fluid economy should push authority for decision making to the people as close to the customer as their capability will allow—then grow the parts of the organization that are devolved while shrinking the parts that are centralized and controlled. This strategy is similar to Waterstones' method of pushing authority out to store managers and shrinking the head office. Alternatively, if there are no obvious devolved parts of the organization, plant parts of the organization that are inverted by utilizing a start-up seeding process such as our Improvisational Innovation methodology described earlier in the book. In this way, it will be possible to create organizations that are responsive both to the needs of your customers and your people.

Do you see the light? Are you looking up for enlightenment or over your shoulder out of fear?

CHAPTER 4

RISK-TAKING LEADERSHIP

When Steve Jobs returned to Apple in 1997 to execute what became one of the most successful turnarounds in corporate history, he made a decision that the company would focus on consumer and business desktops and laptops. His goal was to focus on building the best products in these market spaces, and Jobs became ruthless in this pursuit. Prior to Jobs' return, while most of Apple's businesses floundered, Apple still had an excellent and profitable franchise selling printers. Most people in the Apple printing group assumed that they would be spared the savage cuts that the rest of the company was experiencing, but they were wrong—dead wrong. The entire printer group was eliminated in a single act to ensure the company focused on the strategic items that Jobs had articulated as priorities.

After Jobs gained dominance in the desktop and laptop space, he pondered what to do next. In this environment and under his strong—some might say heavy-handed and narcissistic—leadership, it might seem that launching a consumer-electronics product was somewhat risky. But that is exactly what Tony Fadell did when he joined Apple in 2006.

Fadell, hired as the senior vice president for hardware and mobile devices, is a decisive guy who likes to tinker and invent. In an interview with Saurabh Gupta, who served under Fadell as the engineering manager for iPod software from 2006–12, Gupta recalled how Fadell challenged his team to the biggest engineering achievement—to fit audio processing into a small and sleek device.[1] The iPod, which Fadell quickly became known as the creator of, "was not on plan to have the success that it did and certainly not generate more than 50 percent of Apple's revenue in 2006," according to Gupta, but it did. "Steve thought the iPod would serve as some small accessory for the Mac, not as [a] standalone product," says Gupta. "I think we were all amazed by the response . . . it was such a gamble . . . and because early iPod prototypes looked similar to an early smart phone, we knew that we were on to something else," he continues. That early something became the prototype for the iPhone. What was something of a random and risky attempt to break ground in a new market drove Apple to become the richest company in the world.

Fadell went on to lead the team that designed the first eighteen generations of the iPod and also led the team that built the first three generations of the iPhone. What enabled Fadell to be so experimental was a collage of many things, but most importantly, Jobs gave Fadell total freedom over technical elements, product design, and development, and then Jobs would laser in on the marketing and packaging to complete it. They were a dream team, despite their fourteen-year age difference.

Today, with the benefit of perfect hindsight, we know that the iPod was a huge hit. We can tell that this was the perfect product in the convergence of computers and personal entertainment. But that was far from clear at the time. Some of the comments that were posted on Mac Rumors, an Apple fan blog, just after the iPod's release were:

> The reality distortion field is starting to warp Steve's mind if he thinks for one second that this [iPod] thing is gonna take off.

> Who gets that thing is a very stupid person.

Many complained about the high price tag, but the main complaint was that instead of sticking to what Apple did best—computers—the company had strayed into the consumer-goods market. Looking back, had Apple stuck with computers, there is no doubt that they would not have entered the music-player market or the smartphone market and would now not be the most valuable company in the world.

The ability to embrace risk is critical if leaders are to succeed in the long run. It may not always be clear at the time that there will be a home run, but unless a leader is willing to take some risk, it will be impossible for them to feel the exhilaration of victory. The stark reality is that if leaders don't take risks with developing new products, ideas, and thinking, their organizations will lose market share and relevance or, even worse, become obsolete. Consider the fact that since 2000, 52 percent of Fortune 500 companies have disappeared, and in 2020, 75 percent of the Standard and Poor's index will be companies you have not even heard of yet.

You Have to Trust

One of the greatest challenges in business today is the lack of trust that permeates an organization, but to be a company that survives and grows in the fluid economy, you have to have trust. In their book *The Trusted Advisor,* authors David Maister, Charles Greene, and Robert Galford articulated the trust equation.[2] The factors that determine the level of trust that someone feels toward you can be summarized, according to authors

$$\text{Trust} = \frac{\text{Credibility} + \text{Reliability} + \text{Intimacy}}{\text{Self-Orientation}}$$

Credibility is the background that you bring to the situation that makes it more likely that you have a competitive advantage. For example, Deborah was a credible cofounder and CEO of Betty-Confidential, an online site for women, as she was living a lot of the content offered on the site.

Reliability is a measure of how frequently you've been right in the past. Those who have a long track record of consistently good results are more likely to be trusted than those who don't have this kind of track record.

Intimacy is a measure of how close your relationship is. All other things being equal, we're more likely to trust a dear friend or our spouse than someone whom we've never met.

Self-orientation carries the most leverage in that if you dedicate yourself to the service of others rather than yourself, you are more likely to be trusted. In other words, you are more likely to believe a Mother Teresa than a convicted con man, even on a topic where neither hold particular expertise. Self-orientation can manifest itself in more mundane, day-to-day interactions. Listening carefully and actively is a skill cultivated by many and is one way of demonstrating that you are focused on the interests of people other than yourself. Trying to do even small things for other people whom you interact with is a way in which it is possible to demonstrate your external orientation and thus allows you to increase the level of trust that others will be willing to place in you.

It is notable that reliability and intimacy usually take a lot of time to establish. Typically, people who have these qualities are going to be people whom you have known for a long time and who are like you. And herein lies the problem. If you typically trust the people whom you have known a long time and are similar to you and think the way that you do, how will you come up with something truly innovative? How will you do anything different?

Compare this with a typical hierarchical company, where being seen as a "company man" or "company woman," potentially for decades, would be a prerequisite to being entrusted with the reins of a major new initiative. Decades of performance management would drive you toward the norms of the company in terms of what to do and how you do it—and only those who conform to the norms of the company are likely to be promoted. It is perhaps unsurprising that large, hierarchical companies often struggle to come up with ideas that are innovative and fresh. We now require risk-taking leaders who are ready to trust people who haven't been forged into the mold of the company or who are outside the norm of what people expect in that environment. When leaders are willing to take risks on new ventures that may be different from what they are used to, only then can we deliver the types of innovation that lead to company growth and prosperity.

This will require placing one's faith in people who are scrupulously honest but may have a very different worldview from your own. Thomas Edison was famous for having been homeschooled after a teacher called him "addled" (mentally unsound) on account of his free thinking, nonconformist ways. Conformity and inventiveness are necessarily opposite poles of the personality spectrum. Leaders will have to learn how to embrace these risks, inculcate trust, and engage in creative risk taking.

Set-Based Thinking and the Portfolio of Ideas

When Edison developed the lightbulb, he didn't settle on a single risky idea. He gathered a team together, put them in his lab, did a few theoretical estimates to understand the correct parameters of a potential solution, and then asked his team to test *thousands* of alternative ideas. Edison had only limited understanding of material science; he knew that most of what he tried would fail. Therefore, his safeguard was to have enough experimental options that one of those experiments would lead to a successful outcome.

In 1984, when it looked as though Japanese automakers were about to dominate that very American business—the automotive industry—the US government commissioned a study on the differences between the way American automotive companies designed cars and the way that Japanese companies designed cars. They knew that American automakers took more than twice as many man-hours to design a new vehicle (3.1 million man hours in the United States as compared to 1.7 million for Japanese automotive companies).[4] Additionally, Japanese producers did so with smaller teams (485 employees vs. 903 for American companies) and in less time (46.2 vs. 60.4 months). So why was this? What was the underlying cause of the increased efficiency of the Japanese automakers vs. American ones?

One of the big differences was that Japanese automakers embraced set-based concurrent engineering. At the time, US automotive designers would come up with several proposals for the design of, say, an air-conditioning vent. The US designer would then immediately settle on one choice and proceed to engage in detailed design work. Once all the detailed designs for all the parts were complete, then and only then would there be an attempt to integrate all the pieces. What inevitably followed was the realization that several of these detailed designs would not fit together or not work together as a system. As such, the designer would either have to engage in the laborious process of redesigning his concept at a detailed level or wait for someone else to do so before the entire design team could move on to the next step. The end result was that there was extensive waiting and delay.

Contrast this with the Japanese's approach of set-based concurrent engineering. If the Japanese automakers were designing a similar part, they would typically come up with many concepts, perhaps a dozen. Then the Japanese automakers would discuss these concepts within the broader engineering team to see which ones would work best in the final system. Over time, the team would narrow down the number of options that they would develop, but the point is they would maintain several options at all stages before going final. Finally, they might do detailed designs and prototypes of potentially several concepts for full-scale design integration. Because of the continued communication and the endless designing, checking, and redesigning, this final integration tended to have many fewer problems, many fewer difficulties, and it ultimately enabled the Japanese designers to achieve success faster.

Maintaining a set of alternatives may seem like a costly activity, but if it is done correctly, it actually saves effort because the cost of failures is typically high.

Apple understood this when they developed and released iPods. Apple maintained an annual release process, usually in September, and they frequently touted how their iPods were 20 percent thinner than the previous generation. This was by design.

In the first few months of their development process, Apple would do full buildups of several different versions of the product. Often, they would maintain a set of alternatives; for example, they would have iPods of different thicknesses, some the same thickness as the previous year's model, some 10, 20, or even 40 percent thinner. Frequently, they would design into their product parts from different suppliers. Having attempted full buildups of different alternatives for the iPods, they were then able to evaluate them and continue to develop various different approaches. They would maintain these alternatives until it became clear that those alternatives would not work or were not necessary—for example, a model with the same thickness as last year's model is redundant if you are certain a thinner one will work.

As they went through the year, the iPod development team would pare down the number of different types that were under investigation; very often, several of these alternatives were maintained right through the development cycle until production. In one instance, they maintained in their design process two different alternatives for touch chips (the microchips that control the touchscreen interface). In a departure from previous years, Apple included an FM radio in one of their iPod models. The FM radio and the touch interfaces tended to operate with similar frequencies. It emerged that while listening to the FM radio, at times you could hear a quiet hiss in the background from the touch-interface chip. One of the vendor's chips was reprogrammable and the other was not, and thus, because they had alternatives, Apple was able to reprogram one of the touch interfaces to solve the background noise problem and still release their iPod to market without delay. They might not have been able to do so if they hadn't, early on, set themselves up to explore alternatives.

Thus, it is important when taking risks to maintain a portfolio of alternatives proportionate to the estimated risk so as to ensure success. As we discuss in the chapter on the Improvisational Innovation process, Improvisational Innovation yields many businesses that give you alternatives should one or the other fail. Let's face it, if you are doing something innovative, some of your businesses should fail. Managing risk is an important part of how to be a good risk-taking leader, and this can pay off both in terms of avoiding failure and in terms of increased learning. With multiple attempts at an area, you tend to learn more about that area.

The People Equation Prescription

Any decision that is made to start a new venture or enter a new market involves many factors. If it was a thousand years ago, you were the son of a baker, and you were about to start your own bakery business, perhaps you would be in a position to understand most of those factors. The likely market size in your town, the price of flour, and the cost to turn that flour into a loaf of bread might all be known and understood. Today, however, the situation is rather different. You are fortunate if some of those factors are known in advance, but some will not be. As we move to the fluid economy, and the routine transactions of everyday life become standardized, the only businesses that will remain as open niches will be ones where the very factors that the business depend on will be necessarily unknown. Many of the important factors may be highly ambiguous; it may even be difficult to know what the important factors are. As such, any business venture has to be one that involves risk—risk that stems from what we don't know about the business we are entering, or what we don't know we need to know. Just as when the iPod was released, it was far from clear it would be a success. But in a world of unknowns, how can you take risk? What can you do that enables you to embrace risk but ensure success?

Risk-taking needs to be at the heart of your leadership. Embracing risk is vital to enable the exploration of ideas that otherwise might seem absurd, and it is only through embracing risk that one can do something truly novel. After all, if the outcome were known, it wouldn't be new.

You actually can't do or say anything useful without taking risk. For example, if someone asked me if the weather might be suitable for a walk, I could say yes, which would risk being wrong but would lead to a clear decision as to what to do. In the alternative, I could say the probability of it raining is somewhere between 0 and 100 percent—an entirely accurate statement that is completely without utility and adds no value.

Because of the rate of change in the fluid economy, managing risk and making it safe to take risks are critical components of the leadership style that is required. This means that leaders must acknowledge the risks that people in an organization face and accept the fact that failures are part of this process. For your people to perform at their best, they must have a sense of psychological safety, so it is up to the leader to set the tone that risk and failure are okay. Only if the leader has embraced risks and shows comfort with failure will your people feel safe enough to share ideas.

Think like a chief innovation officer, not a chief executive officer. If execution can be largely automated, it's innovation that counts. What this means is that your role as a leader should be to stimulate, gather, and support innovative ideas throughout the company. Here in Silicon Valley, CIOs and VCs spend their time enabling innovators even if they don't do the innovation themselves. Given this, they are always on the hunt for good ideas that they can propel forward. What is also true is that the whole organization should be focused not just on innovating but on propelling the innovations of others forward. Only then can those innovations flourish and bear fruit.

Twenty percent of your team should be risk takers. In a top-down, leader-focused company, it's tempting to embrace only those people who reflect the leader or a standard template. This monotonous repetition of a standard cutout "company man" or "company woman" can cause things to run efficiently from the leader's perspective, but it will not enable success for the company when change is the norm. Instead, 20 percent of your people should be bold risk takers—people who break the mold. It's not necessary for all your people to be so keen to do things differently, but unless a healthy portion of your people are the types that do this, your team will be less innovative and less effective. Ultimately, you need both innovation and execution.

Focus on value creation over immediate profits. Both Silicon Valley VCs and wise investors look for companies that are creating value over companies that have short-term profits. VCs in Silicon Valley frequently back companies that, for example, have no profits but hold a large and growing user base or an impressive patent portfolio. They do this knowing that in the end, these are things that create value and will make them successful. We should measure the efforts of our people and our companies the same way. If a person innovates and creates valuable new ideas, that may be more valuable to the company than the short-term value derived from that person's ability to execute on the topic of the moment. So we should assess, promote, and measure our people on these dimensions.

Provide equity or stock to everyone, because everyone is responsible for the success of the organization. This last prescription is a mindset as much as it is a prescription. The mindset that people who contribute value should be richly rewarded really matters to the long-term success of your organization. What this means is that internal start-ups should reserve a portion of the value that they create for those who created the value. If you don't do this, you are asking your most innovative, most capable, most value-creating people to innovate elsewhere. Once the company has reached a mature size, it is still important to enable broad ownership of the company. There is always an element of shared sacrifice in any functioning company, so there must also be a sense of shared reward. The visceral reminder that you are an owner makes it easier to enable responsible but difficult decisions. When shares and stock are elements of the shared rewards that the company brings—part of the company's culture—the sense of shared responsibility and shared sacrifice thrives. This makes the company more capable of embracing the changes that we will all face.

In the fluid economy, expecting people to be "right" will be a futile exercise—constantly expecting people to accept measured risk is a more useful notion. What this means in practice is that you are going to have to build trust with your people. Trust is the confidence that the individual will act in the best interest of the organization as a whole, even though the organization may not have a full understanding of the issues that the individual is driving. Trust means a belief that if there is a failure of a venture, it's probably not because the person who was involved didn't try their best to make it work; it's because the overall business conditions did not favor that idea.

The fluid future demands that we make people the center of everything that we do. This means that leaders will have to be prepared to take some risks, both with people and with the ventures that they propose. If leaders can't find ways to take measured risks, they will not be able to put forward interesting products. But more importantly, they will not be able to develop and retain their most valuable people.

Are your teams flourishing by reaching for the sky?

CHAPTER 5

THE CORPORATE CULTURE OF HOW

Robert Gore, an American engineer, scientist, and the founder (in 1958) of W. L. Gore & Associates, a multinational manufacturing company, believed in implementing a team-based, lattice-like organizational structure that encourages personal initiatives and communication among all associates, which was quite a departure from the traditional management structures of the time. The privately held company is best known for creating innovative, technology-driven solutions in four areas: electronics, fabrics (such as Gore-Tex and Elixir guitar strings), industrial, and medical products. Today, W. L. Gore employs more than ten thousand people, who are referred to as "associates," not employees.

Within W. L. Gore, there is no traditional organizational chart, no chain of command, and no hierarchical channels of communication. Instead, Gore's leadership believes in communicating directly with one another, enabling each member of their team to be accountable and find personal fulfillment while contributing to the company. Initially, when an associate is hired, they work in general work areas. Then, with the guidance of their sponsors—not bosses—associates explore projects that match their skill set. Gore's efforts to create an environment that offers freedom and autonomy forces leaders to emerge with a specific knowledge, skill, or experience that advances a business objective within the company.

The four principles of W. L. Gore's culture are:

- fairness to each other and everyone with whom they come in contact;

- freedom to encourage, help, and allow other associates to grow in knowledge, skill, and scope of responsibility;

- the ability to make one's own commitments and keep them;

- consultation with other associates before undertaking actions that could impact the reputation of the company.

In an October 2012 *Fast Company* article entitled "Terri Kelly, The 'Un-CEO' of W. L. Gore, on How to Deal with Chaos: Grow Up," Kelly, the firm's current CEO, states that Gore doesn't necessarily focus on driving organizational effectiveness.[1] She says, "I'd rather come at this challenge from the creative side, and then put structures around creativity, than figure out how to build creativity where it didn't exist." She continues, "We have constant debates: Is this overstepping the boundary, is there too much rigidity, we don't want to lose the creativity and energy in the process? But we want to create a broader architecture, a framework." This cultural mindset is what maximizes associates' individual potential while focusing on product advancement and nurturing an environment where creativity is embraced.

"We have what we call rainmakers and implementers," Kelly explains. "Rainmakers come up with wild ideas, implementers make them real. The two drive each other crazy. If you're not careful, control will gravitate to the implementers. So we try to protect the rainmakers. That means we have to be comfortable with more chaos."

Kelly believes that transparency builds trust, and with trust being the number one obstacle that prohibits people from creating and innovating, the formula works well for Gore. They are even comfortable admitting failures and mistakes. In 2006, Medtronic, a premier medical technology and services company, sued W. L. Gore for allegedly infringing on five of the company's patents related to intravascular stents, tiny tubes used to prop open arteries. Instead of avoiding the dispute within the organization, Gore decided to notify the entire company of the occurrence. "Some companies try to keep protected. You end up filtering so much, your people are really disconnected. And the younger generation, especially, is exposed to so much information, they are expecting it not to be filtered. Communities of folks are talking about you. If you try to control it, it will come back to haunt you," says Kelly.

W. L. Gore & Associates is a strong example of a Culture of How, where the focus is not on what you do in business, but how you get things done. How do you enable employees who have good ideas to build upon them in a safe environment and make them great, free from the burden of hierarchy? How do you start from a place of trust and measure results, not by the time on the clock but by creative pursuits, productivity, and overall outcome?

Culture, by definition, is the set of operating principles that people within the organization adopt, whether it is consistent with their value systems or not. People within the organization become indoctrinated into that culture, inevitably learn how best to function within it, and, oddly enough, are resistant to change, usually because of a lack of trust or fear whenever something new or different is introduced. By human nature, people are more comfortable falling back into old habits. Therefore, creating cultural change is just plain difficult, often so problematic that it can be accomplished only in the context of another, larger disruption to the organization, such as in the case of an acquisition or joint venture, which forces cultures to look beyond their daily norms and acumen.

Consider the case of New United Motor Manufacturing (NUMMI), an automobile-manufacturing plant that was jointly owned by General Motors (GM) and Toyota from 1984 until 2010. Prior to the joint venture, NUMMI was a GM-owned plant and had a toxic culture of antagonism between management and assembly workers. There were many accounts of workers' reckless behavior, such as deliberately starting fires in the plant on game night so that production would be halted and workers could make it to the ball game on time. Even more damaging were the cases of workers knowingly injecting defects into cars on the assembly lines, even defects that could be hazardous to drivers. The product quality and productivity of the NUMMI plant was the worst in the GM network, and management tried to change the culture in the factory, but eventually, after years of poor performance, the plant was closed down and all the employees were laid off. After the joint venture between GM and Toyota was agreed to, the same plant was reopened a short while later as NUMMI. Surprisingly the new Toyota management hired back all the same employees that were there when the plant was a poorly performing plant owned solely by GM. Because the plant had gone through a major disruption, cultural change was not only possible but also embraced. NUMMI went from being the worst-performing plant in the network to the best. Relations between the union workforce and management remained good right up to when the plant was again shuttered after the Great Recession of 2008. For so many companies like Toyota in the 1950s and General Motors in 2008, cultural change was deemed improbable until their respective companies were threatened with bankruptcy. So very often, a massive disruption is required to clearly communicate that the old rules no longer apply.

In our innovation practice at Vorto Consulting, we look for a disruption that we can leverage to inject the cultural change an organization requires to survive and then thrive. Sometimes our change activity is happening in the context of a reduction in workforce, something that is always regrettable—and rarely something that we seek—but almost always effective in enabling the organization as a whole to start to think differently about their operating modes.

Disruption is often required, but it is by no means enough. Risk-taking leadership and role modeling, which we discuss later in the book, are essential, but more than these, learning and embracing some of the tools that are required for the future culture are also important. Often, we get organizations that cascade their training downward. In this form of deployment, the senior leader trains the people below him and they train the people below them. This does two things:

- It ensures that the leaders fully grasp the concepts of the training; rarely will someone feel comfortable offering training on something they themselves don't fully grasp. Asking leaders to train means that they pay attention during their training and equip themselves to be good role models. This is why it is well known that the act of training others usually results in retaining more than simply attending the training yourself.

- It communicates an underlying message to the leader's subordinates that the concepts are going to be taken seriously, and it explicitly starts the conversation between the leader and the subordinate as to how the principles can be put into action.

In the People Equation, you have to create a culture that embraces people to be their best, authentic selves and, in the process, display a willingness to play ball with others. It is about embracing people's uniqueness rather than focusing on someone's education or cultural characteristics such as gender, height, appearance, ethnicity, level of experience, age, and the like. Instead, how about focusing on a person's passion, core expertise, interests (how they spend time outside the office), and different mindsets?

Research by Dan Cable, a professor of organizational behavior at the London Business School, shows that employees who feel welcome to express their authentic selves at work exhibit higher levels of organizational commitment, individual performance, and propensity to help others.[2] For far too long, we have focused on people who look like us, went to school where we went, have similar handshakes or modes of eye contact, and have like-minded intellectual abilities. However, these commonalities are not measurable when looking at someone's potential to bring big ideas to the table. If they were, it is likely that you would have passed on bringing an Albert Einstein into your organization. In 1895, at sixteen years of age, Einstein applied for early admission to the Swiss Federal Polytechnic School (Eidgenössische Technische Hochschule, or ETH) in Zurich and failed the entrance exam. He passed the math and science sections of the exam, but he performed abysmally on the rest of it, on subjects such as history, languages, and geography. Einstein actually had to go back to high school before he retook the exam and was finally admitted to ETH a year later, according to Dr. Karl Kruszelnicki at ABC Science.[3] Even after his college education, Einstein wasn't good enough to receive a professorship and ended up being a third-rate assistant examiner at the Federal Office for Intellectual Property in Bern, Switzerland. It was not until 1911 that Einstein became a full professor at the German Charles-Ferdinand University in Prague.

The People Equation Prescription

A Corporate Culture of How refrains from placing judgment on the characteristics of people who are unlike you and embraces a plurality of differences. To do this, you need a method to inculcate this practice. Typically, in a hierarchical organization, you do this by creating a vision, mission, values, and strategy statement that would be directed by the top of the organization and promulgated throughout the hierarchy. In a Corporate Culture of How, you lead solely with your values—not through a traditional mission statement—and through informal norms that can be discussed and integrated continuously. Once those values are clearly understood and embraced, you can expect and enable the following:

Start from a place of trust until you have reason not to trust. We addressed the issue of trust in preceding chapters, and we can't underscore it enough. Trust is the one characteristic that will make or break an organization. Yet the importance of establishing trust is rarely practiced. We believe there is nothing more important than trust in a fluid economy.

When Deborah was teaching innovation process (and stressing the importance of trust) to a group of fifty manufacturing CEOs at an executive education program at Tecnológico de Monterrey in Lyon, Mexico, one of the participants said to Deborah, "We don't even trust one another in this room, so how do you expect us to collaborate?" Deborah responded by offering two choices: you can do nothing and continue to lose market share (in this case, it was shoe manufactures who were losing market share to the Chinese), or you can establish a new mindset for how people can work together. Pick one person and collaborate, starting from a place of trust (until you have reason not to), and be the model for others to follow.

Twenty percent participation. "It has been my observation that if you invite an entire business unit, division, or enterprise to innovate, at any one time, 20 percent of the people will be engaged in some form of innovation activity (e.g., thinking up new ideas, working on business cases, developing prototypes), " says Laszlo Gyorffy, a principal at Enterprise Development Group.[4] He continues, "While 20 percent may not sound like a lot, it is usually the amount of change that an enterprise can handle. I would also say the 20 percent number is fluid in terms of who are the people contributing. In other words, the percentage may stay the same, but different people participate at different times. I believe everyone has the potential to come up with a good idea." In many cases, an employee may think, "I may have a big idea and work on it from January to April this year, but then not take anything new on for months," according to Laszlo. With Laszlo's point in mind, we have found that there are serial "intrapreneurs" in most organizations. These are the people who see a problem or an opportunity and cannot help themselves, as they must solve the problem or capture the opportunity. These are the people who are always championing something and should be nurtured and supported in a way that they can safely carry out their ideas, free from the fear of being criticized, micromanaged, or let go. These are the core entrepreneurial, risk-taking types who provide consistent fuel to the company's innovation engine.

Twenty percent time. Allow people to step away a day a week or for 1.5 hours each day to explore and tinker with new ideas that may or may not have anything to do with their daily job. In a fluid economy, no one is immune from disruption and anyone can get into your line of business even though they may not currently be in your business. Your employees have to reflect on new ideas, incremental improvements, and perhaps the next big idea. In our anecdote about Apple in the preceding chapter, it was not anticipated that a computer company would evolve into a consumer-electronics company, and it certainly was an unexpected surprise how well the iPod was adopted by consumers across the globe. Had Tony Fadell and his team not had the freedom and time to experiment, to test out numerous prototypes that failed and then won, we wouldn't be enjoying the iPod today. Encourage people to get out of the office, breathe fresh air, and spend time doing something they enjoy doing, but set up a process that will capture their ideas or improvements, such as Improvisational Innovation discussed in chapter 2.

Promote networking within and build on ideas. One of the greatest challenges of large organizations is the difficulty of having their employees network with other employees outside an employee's division or area of work. This is an enormous loss to everyone's potential because by cross-pollinating various skill sets and passions, there is a tremendous opportunity for people to learn from one another.

A Corporate Culture of How fosters an ideation process in which people who don't work together day to day should have the opportunity to come together and build on ideas. In Deborah's book *The Risk Factor*, she covered NetApp, a data-storage company that encouraged employees to think about new ideas and allowed them to bring their ideas to other divisions to seek ways to improve their ideas before they brought them to their own divisions for approval and budget.

The language of "Yes, and . . ." Also in *The Risk Factor*, Deborah wrote about David running the robotics Hacker Dojo in Mountain View, California, where a group of robotics hobbyists gathered to build robots on the weekend. This all-volunteer group met on Saturdays and included a variety of interesting people: a former NASA scientist, a senior engineer who wrote some of the most difficult software present on some of the earliest computer workstations, a precocious software engineer who had already started his own consulting company before he had reached his teenage years, and, among many others, a retired Lockheed-Martin satellite guidance systems engineer. The team, while all enthusiastic, faced a significant challenge: robots, without a good guidance system, don't know where they are.

The retired Lockheed engineer had an idea for how to solve this problem. Satellites solve a similar problem by looking at patterns of stars. He reasoned that in the same way, the robot could look at lights on the ceiling and thereby figure out its location. After a couple of weeks of effort, the Lockheed engineer came back with some kind of light sensor mounted on a piece of wood, with part of a plastic bottle painted black attached to this setup. As David looked at the handiwork, he was thinking, "This is clearly never going to work," but instead of sharing this unhelpful immediate reaction, he thought about the concept of "Yes, and . . . ," took a deep breath, and said: "Okay, so what's the next step?"

The engineer discarded the painted plastic bottle pretty quickly, but he just as quickly came up with a system based on off-the-shelf cameras. A few weeks later, David was watching in amazement as the Lockheed engineer was demonstrating a system that could provide centimeter-accurate feedback based on ceiling lights.

If humans are predisposed to respond negatively to innovative ideas—when the people putting forward those ideas are most vulnerable and most likely to be damaged by rejection. The emotion of denial—which often leads to "no"—can feel harsh to someone who has just put themselves in the vulnerable position of putting forward a new idea. The emotion of anger is necessarily threatening for someone who would otherwise continue to engage his or her whole cerebrum in a thoughtful process of envisioning a better future. Compromise can often be perceived as watering down a vigorous idea. Depression or other displays of negativity can only dampen the embers that may ignite a new idea. How is an innovation-oriented individual to respond? I call it the language of "Yes and. . . ."

In the language of "Yes and . . . ," when you are greeted with a new idea, you respond in the affirmative and then try to redirect or build on the idea in a way that makes it more productive for the organization. This does two things:

- It helps integrate the idea into your own thinking. The notion of "Yes and . . ." is a useful device to force you to consider fully how you can make use of the idea. It doesn't eliminate the possibility of eventual rejection, but it allows you to direct the emotions of rejection toward analyzing the concept and trying to make it better.

- It encourages the suggestor to come up with a further, richer, more deeply held idea that can enable further progress.

What comes after "and . . . ?" Your "and . . ." should try to encapsulate any concerns that you have about the idea and suggest a next step that will enable the idea to move as far forward as it genuinely has legs to do so.

Innovation is a vulnerable place because it is intrinsically an uncertain place. As we've mentioned before, if you knew what the outcome would be, it wouldn't be innovation. Also, obvious solutions are clearly not game-changing innovations, and truly innovative solutions are not obvious. This combination means that the most natural reaction in the world is to say no, but this is also the response that is most destructive to stimulating further innovation.

"For an idea that does not at first seem insane, there is no hope." — Albert Einstein

Innovation always requires exploring new and unproven territory. By its very defin'ition, innovation implies driving into a space beyond which all previous innovators have gone. If one is innovative, one is always trying for something that has never been done—or trying something that others have attempted but failed. Frequently, the initial attempt of an idea is without merit, but in the act of trying, one might stimulate others to have ideas that are sometimes slightly more worthy than the initial concept.

These ideas may give rise to other, still better ideas, and so it is often only through the vigorous pursuit of many unworthy ideas that a good idea is found. Even then, it is only with great fortune that you come across a successful idea that can really surpass all that has gone before. The process is risky, difficult, and fraught with dangers.

Given these overwhelming odds, what are the chances that someone who is attempting to come up with something new puts forth a new idea that is actually worthy? In addition, if the idea is truly innovative and truly reaches for areas that are uncharted, how is it possible to know definitively whether the idea is good or not? To quote Einstein, "For an idea that does not at first seem insane, there is no hope."

Those who engage in this process are necessarily going to put forward ideas that lack all merit, with the hope that they put forward ideas that merely seem at first to be stupid but have some grain of hope. It is very easy to criticize these ideas and pounce on the vulnerability that putting forward these ideas generates. But to do so would cause that individual to never take that type of risk again, and it will come across as a threat that shuts down open thinking, closing the cerebrum to the very best thinking.

Was the four-minute mile an unbreakable barrier or was it a barrier of the mind?

CHAPTER 6

IT ONLY TAKES ONE

For thousands of years, the four-minute mile was considered an unbreakable barrier. Ancient Greek trainers had fought hard to break this barrier. They supplemented the meat- and fish-rich diet they fed their (much celebrated) athletes with lion's milk in an attempt to build greater strength, but to no avail. The ancient trainers even resorted to having wild beasts and raging bulls chase their athletes to get them to run faster. It did not work. The ancients concluded that breaking the four-minute mile was impossible. They theorized that the human lung had inadequate capacity and that wind resistance was too great. Another theory was that attempting such a feat would actually be dangerous, that the heart would fail at the attempt and bones would shatter and muscles tear from the skeleton as one pushed for such a great exertion. These theories were widely believed well into the modern era of athletics. Yet, right after World War II, a world record in the mile was set, and for years it stood stubbornly, just 1.4 seconds above the four-minute barrier.

Roger Bannister was a talented British athlete and medical student at Oxford. After a disappointing finish in the 1952 Olympics in Helsinki, Finland, from where he returned sans medal, he set his sights on doing the impossible—a four minute mile—to erase what he saw as the stain of a much-publicized defeat.

For months, he visualized success—what it would be like to run a mile in less than four minutes. In this way, he attempted to create certainty about the outcome. He was analytical and determined in his training. Then, he carefully prepared for a small running meet at his home track on Iffley Road in Oxford.

On May 6, 1954, a cool and windy day, the small running track was barely capable of housing the crowd of three thousand that had gathered to watch. When the starting gun sounded, a small group of elite athletes set off on what was to become a historic race. In a preplanned configuration, Bannister ran in between two pacesetters, Chris Chatway, a future Commonwealth Games gold medalist, and Chris Brasher, a future Olympic Games gold medalist. After the first half mile, the first pacesetter was replaced in the lead by the second, and a quarter of a mile later, the second pacesetter also peeled away exhausted. All that was required now was for Bannister to power through to the finish, so he lengthened his stride, and his own pace grew quicker. Bannister was propelled forward by a graceful, flowing rhythm that was a mixture of inborn talent and capability ingrained through years of training. The three-quarter-inch spikes on his running shoes tore through the cinder running track, and in a final motion he leapt for the finish line only to collapse in exhaustion.

The crowd, which had previously been cheering louder and louder as the race went on, fell quiet as they waited for the reading of the time. But the quiet was short lived, as pandemonium erupted when only the first digit of the time was read. Most people in the stadium didn't hear completely the final time of 3 minutes 59.4 seconds.

Perhaps the most striking thing about this record-setting attempt was how quickly it was surpassed, only forty-six days later, by John Landy, an Australian, who ran the mile in a time of 3 minutes 58 seconds. As news of Bannister's and Landy's triumphs circulated, within a year and a half, several athletes had broken the four-minute barrier. It is clear that the barrier was mostly a barrier of the mind.

What It Takes to Act

In large hierarchical institutions, it is difficult to imagine anyone but the chief executive moving the entire company in any given direction. However, as the Roger Bannister story illustrates, in nonhierarchical groups, it takes only one person for others to follow, believe, and act. For people to act, they need to believe several things:

- there is a benefit;
- they have the opportunity to seize this benefit;
- given the opportunity, they have the capability to get that benefit.

Many people fail to believe that getting somewhere is possible, and this belief has the potential to hold people back. The capable runners who were seemingly incapable of breaking the four-minute barrier until they knew that Roger Bannister had done it fall into that class. And this belief is so pervasive within our organizations that many people are beaten down to believe that they can't take the lead. Indeed, hierarchical organizations are designed to cultivate this feeling. In a hierarchical organization, there is only one overall leader, and because most people will never be in that role, this system creates the sense that rising up to the very top is not possible. But that feeling is not a requirement or even important for the sort of people-centric organizations we advocate, where leadership comes from the front line and being the overall chief isn't as important. It almost always takes only one individual to lead others to the realization that something is possible.

The Power of Examples

As we shared earlier, David stands at 6'9" and, as a former rower at Oxford University, still has noticeable calluses on his hands.

David earned the honor to go through the Olympic trials in 2004, but of more interest to Deborah is how David changed his mind-set to push through the rigorous training to believe that anything is possible, and inevitably to succeed at an audacious goal.

David recalls, "When I trained as a rower, we would line up on rowing machines, from fastest on the left to slowest on the right. We'd race through our anaerobic threshold to the point where every muscle in our bodies cried out for oxygen, and the body tells the mind that this can't continue any longer. . . . It was brutal and tested not just the physicality of what my body was capable of, but like so many athletic pursuits, became more mental than anything else."

When David started rowing, his times improved until he occupied the left-most spot in the lineup, where the fastest rowers sat. While his times were exceptionally strong, they didn't keep improving, being perhaps a second faster on some days but not others. Then, one day, a younger, 6'8" powerhouse of a rower appeared in the boathouse.

Instantly, David found himself occupying the second slot from the left, with times that were five seconds slower than the top pace. Then, very quickly, things changed. The following week, his time improved. Suddenly, David was able to row five seconds faster, and the next week nine seconds faster, and then the next week nineteen seconds faster than his previous personal best. In the span of just three weeks, his time had gone from that of a good club rower to one that enabled him to qualify for Great Britain's Olympic team trials.

It's unlikely that three weeks, even with intense training, could have resulted in much physiological change, certainly not enough to explain the big change in David's times. The change was all in David's head.

According to David, the belief that improvement is possible and necessary must be visceral and real for change to occur. Sometimes, connecting at an intellectual level is not enough; he knew there were rowers who had faster times than he did, but it wasn't until David was sitting next to such a rower that he could feel the change.

Later on in his professional life, David transformed a semi-conductor wafer factory that had clearly underperformed for years. He spent hours in meeting after meeting reviewing benchmark data that showed the underperformance. The reality was that none of the factory's leadership had the desire to change. Not until reductions in the factory's workforce started did the mindset there change, and the leaders became receptive to doing things that led to better performance and ultimately saved the factory from closure.

The "Only Takes One" Mindset

As with Roger Bannister's four-minute mile—or with David's rowing experience—having an example is a powerful way of unleashing the belief in the possible. For people to act, that belief must extend beyond an intellectual understanding and become an emotional and visceral internalization that something is possible. Seeing with your own eyes someone doing "the impossible" right next to you is an important way to bring together your emotional and intellectual sides so that you can act in a coherent way. Often, without such an example, no action occurs. David spent a long time occupying the left-most spot on the lineup, but his training did not improve his times until an example was presented to him. Roger Bannister spent months visualizing a successful outcome before finally achieving it, and others, who clearly had the physiology to run faster, did so only after they heard of Bannister's example. Examples, more than anything else, short-circuit the need for a lengthy meditation on the future and make the mental move to a future state possible.

Mindset Lesson #1: While physical and system constraints matter, even more important is a mental or emotional factor that is usually decisive when the need is for high performance.

In David's rowing example, there are no bonus plans or large cash payouts. There are no cash rewards for rowing at this level. Each season, however, David's coach set individualized targets for each rower, known as the *champagne target*—so called because those who got there won a decent bottle of champagne. The target was invariably designed so that the rower would end the season three to four seconds shy of the goal. In short, the target was *almost* unattainable. It was an unabashed challenge, and the rowers knew it.

The result, as David recalls, was a huge motivational boost for each individual. Each time the individual got closer to the target, it stirred him to put in that last ounce of effort. It was a constant source of discussion to ensure success.

What David found most valuable is that the goal of setting targets was not to incentivize or get to a specific place but to challenge *each individual* to perform at his or her personal best. The challenge was not punitive; there was no downside to not attaining it, no one was going to fail to make a house payment if it wasn't attained. But it was meaningful; having the target be seemingly just beyond reach brought out everyone's best.

Mindset Lesson #2: Progress comes through challenge to be better.

David went on to become a rowing coach himself and teamed up with a former US national rower to coach a crew. These two coaches took on a crew that were not natural athletes, with an interest in transforming them into a crew that within one year was prepared to take on a specific set of summertime races in Cambridge, England.

Like his own coach, David pushed his athletes hard. One rower lost thirty pounds in the first three months of David's brutal training regime, which included plenty of basic cardiovascular fitness as well as training rowers to cope with pushing themselves through their anaerobic threshold. Although the regime was demanding, David was careful to ensure that he kept within himself the idea that his athletes' interests were paramount. He always tried to maintain the idea that he would do the right thing for "his guys" because he knew that in doing so he would make the right decisions about coaching practice.

This did not mean going easy on the training; it meant the reverse—being tough and disciplined because that was the route to greatest satisfaction in what they were trying to accomplish together. Years later, David's former athletes would write to him to say how he changed their life and that they were still training.

Mindset Lesson #3: Transforming mindsets can and should mean driving hard, but you must always do so in the context of what you care about and what's best for the individual being changed.

For Roger Bannister, the individual effect of his public failure at Helsinki is what drove him to do what was thought to be impossible. For David, champagne targets were individually set. If the challenge does not fit the individual, it is likely that it will not be effective for that individual. The purpose of the People Equation has to be goals for individual people, too.

We Are All Products of Our Environment

Examples are important because they represent everything that has happened before us. Herbert Spencer, the famed British sociologist and philosopher, asked, "Given a Shakspeare, and what dramas could he have written without ... the various experiences which, descending to him from the past, gave wealth to his thought ... ?"[1] A more modern example might be Steve Jobs. When Jobs dropped out of Reed College, he hung around and dropped in on courses that interested him. At the time, Reed College had the best calligraphy instruction in the country. "Every poster, and every label on every drawer was beautifully hand calligraphed," according to Jobs. He decided that he wanted to learn how to do calligraphy, so he attended classes and learned about serif and sans-serif typefaces and about varying space between different letters. He learned "about what makes great typography great. It was beautiful, historical, artistically subtle in a way that science can't capture," said Jobs.[2]

All this learning was built into the Macintosh ten years later, and because of this, the Macintosh came to dominate desktop publishing. In a more modern version of Herbert Spencer's original question, we might ask, "Would Steve Jobs have been successful in presenting one of the world's more successful desktop publishing systems had he not been brought up in Silicon Valley, had access to integrated circuit components, and learned about calligraphy at Reed College?"

We are all the result of our environment, and because of this, we must create within the organizations we want to breathe life into examples for people to follow. Only if we do this can we stimulate the creation of greatness in the people in that organization to make them effective. If the goal of our organizations is to reach for greatness, we must set up the organization so that our people are given the antecedents that will help them achieve greatness.

Pioneers who can show the way are an important influence that helps people mature to greatness. Pioneers like Roger Bannister help create breakthrough thinking because they make the change that we want to see visceral and real. Pioneers also represent and, to an extent, pass on all the influences that went before them and so enable greatness.

Humans without Limits

How great can greatness be? The "great" ancient Greek cities of the eighth century BC had a population of less than a million, which represented the greatest sphere of influence that any contemporary person could have. A thousand years ago, a "great" king might have had influence over the lives of perhaps one or two million people. Modern corporations, however, can touch the lives of billions. Both Google and Facebook, for example, have products with more than a billion regular users. In other areas of human endeavor, the capacity of modern people is far in excess of those who came before us. This is partly the result of access to technology and partly our superior knowledge.

Today, an experienced yachtsman can readily cross the Atlantic; in fact, this has been done single-handedly even by high schoolers. But only five hundred years ago, it was a feat that would have been the domain of a major national effort. Today, a high-school student can perform acts of computation on his or her cellphone that would have been inconceivable even to the most gifted mathematician but a century ago. High-school students today have sent balloons to the edge of our atmosphere and built rockets that can fly kilometers in the air. We are quite certain that a hundred years from now, when the fluid economy is in full swing, high-school kids will be doing things that today are inconceivable even to the most gifted. This is why we hold out hope that ultimately, there is no limit to the capacity of human beings. It is the nature of people to reach for the stars and achieve greatness. However, sailing across the Atlantic, sending balloons or rockets to the upper reaches of our atmosphere, or performing acts of computation would not be possible today without the role models who accomplished these acts before us. Whatever feats people are doing routinely a hundred years from now will surely be the result of role models who are alive today.

The People Equation Prescription

Because the goal in a people-centric enterprise is to deemphasize the senior leader, it is important to enable peer-oriented role models. It is important to create an environment in which those peer-oriented role models can emerge. Those pioneers must be highlighted and individually honored, not primarily to stimulate them, but to encourage others. It will be better to have a company with thousands of possible role models and pioneers than one with a small number who sit in hierarchically superior positions above employees. In this way, we will be able to create an environment that will enable people to do things that are inconceivable for us today. And as a result, we will be able to explore the unlimited nature of human potential.

Simply put, elevating your best risk-taking mavericks is an important part of an innovative culture. Shifting to this culture will require role models, training, and disruption as we describe in chapter 5 on the Culture of How. However, turning your mavericks into role models is something that should be actively supported. It is important to devote energy to finding and emphasizing the activities of role models, promoting them, and putting them in senior positions. Allowing them to lead, despite their disruptive tendencies, is something that can stimulate people to step out of their day-to-day activities and do the extraordinary.

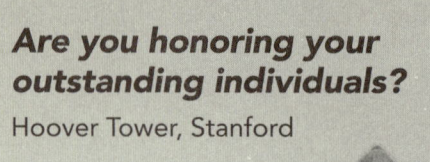

Are you honoring your outstanding individuals?

Hoover Tower, Stanford

CHAPTER 7

MOVING BEYOND THE COMFORT ZONE

In 2007, Brian Chesky and Joe Gebbia, two industrial designers who couldn't pay the rent, decided to put together a simple website to rent out a couple of airbeds in their loft, with the promise of a home-cooked breakfast. They timed their offering for the start of a design conference and called their site "air bed & breakfast." Their initial efforts met with limited success, booking three rentals for $80 per mattress per night. They continued to develop the concept, bringing on a cofounder to build a more sophisticated web destination.

Friends told them, more or less bluntly, that they should be working on other things as they struggled to keep the operation going. In 2008, to raise money to keep the lights on, Brian and Joe made custom boxes of rebranded Honey O's, calling them "Obama O's." They sold them at the Democratic National Convention in Denver, Colorado, for $40 per box as the "Breakfast of Change." This stunt raised $30,000 to keep their operation going on a shoestring. While their site continued to run, and bookings trickled in, they still didn't have enough revenue to sustain the operation—despite the success of their maverick fund-raising campaign. The moment when they were forced to survive by eating the remaining cereal has been described by the founders as a real low point. Shortly after, however, they got their first round of seed funding from Y Combinator, a well-known Silicon Valley incubation program. This funding allowed them to continue to work on the site. After a name change to what we now know as Airbnb and more work on the site, they were able to get additional funding from Sequoia Capital and Y Ventures in 2009.

Airbnb's real success came when Brian decided to engage in the experience of an Airbnb customer choosing to stay in an Airbnb accommodation. Even though Brian has made enough money to build his own mansion, he's been traveling and living in Airbnb units ever since, and has not yet given up his own apartment. Airbnb has continued to grow, with a valuation now of more than $20 billion.

This example of a start-up with deeply committed individuals at the helm doing whatever it takes to make their idea a reality is the stuff of Silicon Valley legends. But why is it that few people have the vision, discipline, strength, and perseverance to do this?

If you think about where most of us come from, we started in a school where we had teachers who had all the answers. From a young age, we were told what to do and, very often, how to think about things. We were surrounded by rules and taught to obey them. As we reached high school, this trend continued. Even at colleges and universities, there is the general expectation that someone's there who can tell you what the answer is.

Moving into adult life, most people who join a large company have a boss who then directs their activities and describes limitations. There are rewards if you are successful and penalties if you aren't. These are usually structured rules and processes meant to bring about the types of behavior that the company thinks it needs.

Given that most people live in this structured and ordinary life, and have done so for the entirety of their lives, it is little wonder that the notion of undertaking an undirected, entrepreneurial activity seems shocking. It is little wonder that the notion of trying to solve the type of problem that Airbnb solved seems unnatural. By definition, innovation requires doing things differently and defying accepted wisdom. If you know everything that is needed to make a product successful, it cannot be innovative. Most people have never had to deal with this kind of uncertainty, have never had to cope with this kind of hardship, can't conceive of operating outside the lines, and have become soft. The bottom line is that we've trained people in our civilization away from doing the things that innovative start-up activity requires.

So how do we get people out of being comfortable with the structures that society provides? Militaries around the world regularly train people away from some of their civilized tendencies, and the better armies are masters of personal development. They take young men and women who have often led sheltered lives and teach them how to survive and fight in foreign, hostile territories under difficult, often harsh living conditions. One of the key methods they use is the gradual introduction of ever-more difficult challenges, until people are capable of the tough things asked of them.

For example, training may begin with rough camping outdoors. It may move on to camping without visible lighting to minimize the chance of detection. Training may escalate to camping in holes that soldiers have to dig in the ground and doing nighttime patrols and exercises. By the end of the training only a few weeks later, recruits are engaged in a series of activities that would have seemed impossible a short while earlier.

The seemingly gradual introduction of ever-more difficult challenges, along with setting the expectation that people develop and thrive because of it, is important in enabling people to grow and develop. If we are going to have a people-centric enterprise, it is imperative to empower people to engage in new businesses that will expand their horizons and those of the corporation. We better be prepared to offer challenges to our people to enable them to rise to the ultimate challenge of starting a new business. We will have to develop within them the capacity to do what years of cosseting has trained out of them—the ability to engage with the unknown and the will to make something out of it.

The Magic of the $3,000 Budget

For Brian and Joe, the founders of Airbnb, some of their most creative moves were born out of a necessity to perform. They couldn't pay the rent, so they had to find another way to raise cash. One wonders whether we would have Airbnb today if these two designers hadn't been out of work during the great recession. Sometimes, giving your people fewer resources forces them to think creatively about their project. This is why, in chapter 2 on Improvisational Innovation, we recommend giving your teams a budget of only $3,000 or less to deliver a prototype—it forces them to be agile with basic materials.

Hermann Hauser founded the ARM chip company, which designs low-power microprocessors. More than fifty billion ARM-based chips have been sold worldwide. When the company was founded, ARM was competing against much larger, global brands, such as National, Intel, and Motorola. Yet, National Semiconductor no longer exists as a stand-alone company, Motorola has since stopped designing microprocessor cores and instead uses ARM-based designs, and at least in terms of the number of cores shipped, ARM has outstripped Intel. The original device was proposed and designed by two engineers, Steve Furber and Sophie Wilson. How did the work of two engineers from Cambridge, England, come to dominate this critical part of electronics?

Hauser is quoted as saying, "When we decided to do a microprocessor on our own I made two great decisions—I gave them two things which National, Intel, and Motorola had never given their design teams: the first was no money; the second was no people. The only way they could do it was to keep it really simple."[1]

The act of giving resources, while necessary, tends to remove challenges. It means that people have the ability to make things more complicated. It means that you don't develop your people to make the hard, simplifying decisions that lead to long-term success.

What is required is allowing people to be their authentic selves, to remove the rules and allow for the organic. You need to provide an environment where self-motivated inventors can lead themselves and take themselves in their own direction. Contrast this to how things often happen in the corporate world.

Sachs's Story

Despite his slightly boyish appearance, Dr. Jacob Sachs is an accomplished biochemist. At twenty-seven years old, Sachs had an aspiration that he wanted to reach within three years, and with the permission of his boss, he put in months of after-hours effort at his company's lab. He was seeking a scientific solution for a disease that had perplexed him since adolescence. His paternal grandfather, who greatly influenced Sachs's interests as a teenage boy, passed away in 1998 from a malignant tumor of the liver. The loss was particularly shattering for Sachs because, as a child, he spent many weekends with his grandfather after his parents divorced shortly after he turned five. It was at the grandfather's burial that Sachs decided that he was going to dedicate his life to the cause of seeking a preventive therapy for the type of tumor that took his beloved family member. In 2010, Sachs graduated from The Johns Hopkins University with a PhD in biochemistry.

Researching a preventive therapy was not directly part of Sachs's day job, but he was deeply driven to explore scientific methods beyond his day-to-day responsibilities. The company Sachs works for is a large American healthcare company, one that is publicly traded. (Sachs requested that the company's name not be disclosed.) About fifteen months into his research, the biochemist discovered a recombinant anti-MIF (anti-macrophage migration inhibitory factor) antibody that would effectively treat patients with solid malignant tumors. While it isn't the precautionary therapy that Sachs continues to aspire to, his discovery has the potential to cure people who have been diagnosed with life-sentencing tumors.

Sachs took his findings to his manager, who then brought them to the company's executive leadership. The buzz over the therapy led to quick corroboration of his results, and leadership decided to invest in human trials. The lawyers filed a patent for the recombinant anti-MIF, and phase 1 trials occurred with patients recruited in the United States in 2012. Simultaneously, the company also aggressively pursued drug testing and marketing in France and Germany, where they could get government approval more rapidly than through the US Food and Drug Administration (FDA). Within a year of being tested in France, Sachs's drug therapy was brought to market.

In France alone, the drug therapy surpassed its plan for projected revenue of $30 million in 2013, generating more than $55 million. While the company waited for FDA approval, they expanded throughout Western Europe, where the therapy was expected to generate $500 million in revenue in its first two years.

In exquisite detail, Sachs detailed his feelings about his discovery, using phrases such as "euphorically overcome" and "emotionally engulfed." He said, "I am blessed to have chosen the path that I did because I feel most alive playing a small role in eradicating a hideous disease that has perplexed us far too long."[2]

In the eyes of his company, what Sachs did was to unintentionally create a sizable new revenue stream. In an industry where, according to the Tufts Center for the Study of Drug Development, it takes approximately $2.6 billion to bring a new drug therapy to market—where years of research and development are the norm—here was a young biochemist who stumbled upon a life-changing finding on his own time.[3]

For his groundbreaking discovery, Sachs was awarded a bonus of $1,500 and a few more of his company's stock options. Yet not once was Dr. Sachs publicly recognized for his discovery. In fact, at a pharmaceutical industry awards dinner in 2014, it was Sachs's director who accepted recognition for the innovative finding of the antibody. Sachs wrote off the disappointment as part of being a newbie in a traditional and hierarchical industry. In our phone interview, however, he disclosed that he can't help but imagine what it would have been like to make this discovery at a place that valued his contribution, musing about what the outcome might have been if he'd had his own entrepreneurial venture. Sachs said, "It was less about the money and more about the recognition that my work will now have an effect on advancing the fight against cancer. . . . I have to admit, I do lose sleep, feeling as if I have been slighted by the company that told me when they hired me, 'do good work and you will be rewarded.'"

Sachs's narrative is not a new one. Sadly, his story embodies the norm of how companies treat their most valuable employees—the very people who help the company evolve to the next level. Furthermore, what precedent does it set when people like Sachs get such relatively meager financial rewards and little recognition? This type of behavior, common in hierarchical institutions, dooms them to pushing the innovators within their ranks to self-select another path. Fortunately for Sachs's employer, he hasn't left yet, but it doesn't always work out that way. But perhaps what is more damaging about Sachs's story is that the behavior of his employer destroys the mutual trust that is required to make people-centered systems work.

The People Equation Prescription

In a people-centered enterprise, the development of individuals will be paramount for a company to succeed. While it is critical for companies to let loose the bridle so that the horse can run as fast as possible, it's equally important that individuals in that people-centric environment are self-motivated, self-disciplined, and honest.

Unless the individuals who are released to work in a people-centric organization develop those characteristics, it will be impossible to sustain meaningful performance. Failure in any one of those areas will cause underperformance or worse, and the ability to trust will evaporate. And without trust, it will be impossible to take risks, meaning there will be little innovation. Instead, if individuals are constantly challenged in their work, and consistently strive to meet those challenges, then over time trust will rise along with capability in a virtuous circle, and the ability to innovate will increase. A trust-oriented, people-centric environment is the one that we are shooting for, but it starts with a basic commitment to that ideal from employees and the capabilities within them to make it work.

In the People Equation, the goal of the organization is to present challenges to individuals that are often outside their comfort zone, because only then will those individuals develop. For example, to demand creativity in their solution, challenge people to bring a product to market with as few resources as are required. Better still, let and expect them to challenge themselves. Then, when your people rise to the challenge and succeed, you must richly reward them. Let them know that failure is not only acceptable, it is required. Use your commitment to the space between what you know they can do and the greater challenge that you are expecting of them to create trust.

Alley to the Valley summit: where the art of the ask is the foundation of the community.

Are you practicing the art of the ask?

CHAPTER 8

THE ART OF THE ASK

Alley to the Valley started in 2010 in a phone conversation between Deborah and Janet Hansen, the founder of 85 Broads (later known as Elevate Network) and a former executive at Goldman Sachs. Janet asked Deborah, "What is going on with the women in Silicon Valley? Whatever it is, can you bottle it up and send it here to the women on the East Coast?"

Deborah had moved to Silicon Valley from the East Coast in 2006, so she knew exactly where Janet was going. Irrespective of the less-than-flattering media attention given to gender inequity in tech and venture capital, there is a hubris, an ability to push the envelope, and a comfort in being in the driver's seat among Silicon Valley women, making many of them very prosperous in opportunity and wealth. In 2010, many Silicon Valley women were gaining notoriety, reaching heights that many of their East Coast counterparts seemed more challenged to achieve.

Deborah and Janet agreed that whatever the "it" was that gave Silicon Valley women their hubris and a place in the driver's seat was worth learning from. They assembled a group of highly accomplished women—investors, entrepreneurs, corporate executives—from both coasts and met in the ballroom of the Rosewood Hotel in Menlo Park, California, on November 11, 2010. Sheryl Sandberg, COO of Facebook, gave the keynote address, and the *New York Times* covered the gathering. Deborah and Janet called the summit Alley to the Valley—meaning an event that bridged Silicon Alley of the East Coast and Silicon Valley of the

West Coast—but whichever coast you were from, East or West, there was still more to accomplish.

In planning the summit, Deborah was consumed by the content and flow of the day. How should these women spend their time together? Were they willing to share networks? What could these successful women learn from one another? Will there be a return on investment?

Janet repeatedly said to Deborah, "Stop worrying. . . . Having these women in the room with one another will be enough." The one thing we did know was that the summit needed to be intimate, so we limited it to fifty women—twenty-five from the East Coast and twenty-five from Silicon Valley. The women would sit at one large U-shaped conference table to suggest parity, and no matter what, the summit was going to empower a safe, trusted environment where the women could comfortably share what was on their minds. We put two rules on the table: coming to Alley to the Valley was about every other woman in the room, and conversations and collaborations needed to move the needle forward. We also banned two conversations from the room: there would be no discussion about balancing work and family and no denigrating men.

Alley to the Valley was supposed to be a one-time event. Deborah was CEO of a content company, Desha Productions, and going through a formal process of due diligence about a possible exit of one of Desha's business units. Janet was running 85 Broads. Neither of them signed up for what Alley to the Valley was about to become.

After publication of the *New York Times* article on the gathering, titled "The Risk-Taking Edge of West Coast Women,"[1] Deborah was bombarded by interest from other women across the country—women such as Barbara Corcoran (one of the investors on ABC's *Shark Tank*), Jean Chatzky (financial journalist and contributor on the *Today Show*), and a woman who owned a Greek island. Even then-Treasurer of the United States, Rosie Rios, reached out and inquired how to get involved.

Shortly after the first summit, Deborah started to hear about the flow of deals that occurred as a result of the women being in the room together. Maria Cirino, of 406 Ventures in Boston, and Amanda Reed, of Polmar Ventures in Menlo Park, were sharing investment deals. Suzy Ginsburg, of Global Communications Works and an angel investor, sat next to Adrienne Messiels, a tech entrepreneur, at lunch and gave Adrienne her first angel investment. We took great pride in the fact that these women had met and took action at Alley to the Valley.

From there, Deborah and her team rolled up their sleeves and thought, for Alley to the Valley to morph into the proverbial golf course for female deal making, it needed to offer an expanded definition of what "deal flow" is. Deal flow was not just about sharing investment deals; it was also about bringing other industry women into the room to elevate these women's profiles so that they could land opportunities that would help them achieve greater heights. We needed media experts, women in executive search firms, and speaking and literary agents who could help get these highly accomplished women covered in the media, place them on corporate boards and in the C-suite, sign book deals, and serve as keynote speakers. The network would be about who was in the room that day, but also about one, two, or six degrees of separation among other high-achieving women. In other words, Alley to the Valley's secret sauce was to cross-pollinate accomplished women in industry and across geography.

Pamela Ryckman, a freelance journalist and budding author, met her literary agent at Alley to the Valley and got a book deal for *Stiletto Network*. Jennifer Abernathy, the CEO of the Sales Lounge, a social-media company, developed a dozen new clients, which lead to increased revenue for her company. And Martha McGarry, a corporate partner at the law firm of Skadden, Arps, Slate, Meagher & Flom was able to bring Heidi Roizen, a successful Silicon Valley entrepreneur turned venture capitalist, into the vetting process of a Fortune 100 corporate board seat. We were moving the needle in unanticipated ways. No matter how successful, how high-profile these women were, the community would commit to check their egos at the door, get down to work, and admit their struggles—in rapid time. But once their struggles were put forth, the room would focus on a solution—a result for every single woman.

After a few Alley to the Valley summits, we came up with a method that focuses on deal making, where every woman brings an "ask" and an "offer" to the table (it could be raising capital; seeking a strategic partner, exit strategy, or corporate board seat; or needing introductions to a corporate executive, potential clients, literary agent, or reporter; and so on). Because these women came with massive Rolodexes and were either the decision makers or connected to decision makers, we agreed to a mission by which each woman's "ask" is answered and her "offer" taken up that day or shortly thereafter. These ask/offer deal-making sessions were highly effective and created a special bond among the women because they were like-minded and no longer felt as though they were the only woman at the table who wanted something more and may have had difficulty achieving it. The in-person summits and later the online community became about "I need this" and "You need that"—"Can you help me?" and "I will help you." We built a community with this specific ask/offer purpose, and as a result, it was pouring in new opportunities for most every single attendee.

Since the launch of Alley to the Valley, Deborah has been interviewed by reporters who repeatedly ask, "What surprises you the most about these highly accomplished women?" Deborah's response has been consistent from the beginning: "There is a disconnect between next-level goals, knowing what to ask for, and the practice of asking in general." Given that one of the most important lessons we are ever taught is that if you don't ask, you don't get, we are continuously surprised by individuals who question what exactly they are asking for.

In Innovation, the Importance of the Ask

Having an ask is beneficial for the individuals involved because it helps guide them to what it is that they ultimately want to achieve, but the practice of asking is also great for organizations because it provides valuable insights about where people want to head day to day and in their long-term career planning. Certainly, an individual needs to be cognizant of what their ask is, but in a very noisy world, where we have lost the art of asking (our social-media world is more about telling), the practice of asking atrophies.

In Silicon Valley, the introductory question that pervades the culture is "How can I help you?" This very question forces people to get used to a culture of asking. This is not to suggest that everyone in Silicon Valley regularly practices asking, but in a place where the start-up culture dominates the landscape, the entire success of an entrepreneurial start-up depends on whether you are successful at what you ask for. From the moment you build a company, you are asking people for money, asking people to buy into your vision, asking your colleagues to risk financial security, asking for that potential strategic partner to buy a product or service that they may not realize they needed, and so on. People in Silicon Valley often see themselves as a start-up, nimble to pivot and grow in a fluid economy, and it serves them well in most any environment they might explore.

Why is the ask imperative to driving innovation? At its base, an ask is to "say something in order to obtain an answer or some information" or "request (someone) to do or give something," according to Merriam-Webster's dictionary. Without an ask, you cannot propel something forward, nor do you grow, improve on your ideas, and so on. Therefore, "asking" is a critical component of an innovation process. The ask also aids in two seminal outcomes—if it is done in a safe environment and in the right context, where the art of the ask is put into practice. First, someone gets to express what's on their mind in a nonthreatening manner, and a manager—if he or she is in the moment and actively listening—gets the benefit of learning what is on an employee's mind. It gives the manager an opportunity to learn about ideas, thought processes, and how to best develop their talent. Second, the ask has the opportunity to create exponential learning and value. By asking for one thing that may or may not come to fruition, the ask may transform into other opportunities that someone hadn't given thought to, which can be a valuable tool in further developing someone's talents.

Creating a Safe Environment

Today, there is no more important role for a manager than developing an employee's talents, but it has to be done in a safe environment. At Alley to the Valley, we created a safe environment for people to ask and offer. We set the expectation for why the women were at the summit in the first place, and we allocated time for people to ask for what they needed, and a time for people to offer help to others. It is not that highly influential women needed to be segregated from their male counterparts, but for the women at Alley to the Valley, there is still new territory to navigate, and for a majority of our attendees, there is a great comfort in being in the company of like-minded people who have experienced some of the same opportunities and challenges. While at a summit, if a woman blurts out a comment or question that is perceived as risky in other environments, they are more likely to share details because they have a sense that others in the room will shake their heads up and down in agreement—that they too have encountered something similar. There is value in having together in a room compatible people who share unique yet similar experiences.

If you think about it, leadership meets regularly with various business units to solve problems, so why shouldn't other groups get to meet on a semiregular basis to share asks? You can begin with similar peer groups, such as "women's leadership" or "minority STEM" groups, but then cross-pollinate other peer groups so that new settings help an individual grow and learn and understand the vernacular of others' expertise and also help define the likes and dislikes based on the information and ideas that others share.

The People Equation Prescription

The art with which people ask will have a monumental impact on your innovation growth engine. However, to have successful sessions at which people make their requests, you have to put in place a practice and time and have people prepared for what they are asking for. Advise them to do the following:

Know what it is that you ultimately want to achieve and commit. To have an ask, you have to know what it is that people ultimately want to achieve. Have your people document and commit to an annual, semiannual, or monthly goal.

On the Alley to the Valley website (www.alleytothevalley .com), we begin our methodology with a request to document your goal and make a commitment to achieving that goal by signing your name:

I, _____ challenge myself to accomplish the following goals by the following dates.

a. _____ by _____.

b. _____ by _____.

Signed, _____

Develop a blueprint. Additionally, on the Alley to the Valley website, you can see how we developed a blueprint to answer the what, why, where, and how around your ask. The blueprint is a personal strategic plan that addresses the goal and the steps that you need to follow. You need to know why you hold this goal and how it will benefit and impact others. Your plan will reflect your thinking about key elements that will guide your current and future actions. Once you have clarity about your specific goal, you will be able to sell your objective more effectively. Consider the following questions:

- Mission and purpose. Why are you striving for this goal?

- Value proposition. How will your goal benefit others?

- Target audience

- Decision makers. Identify and list the people who have decision-making authority or others who can help you achieve what you want.

- Competitive advantages

- Challenges to success

- Differentiator. What is different about you that will enable you to accomplish your goal, where others have failed?

Test your ask out on others first and run scenarios. Before making an ask, test it out on at least three people, such as a significant other, friend, and trusted colleague. You need to know how your ask sounds, appears, and fits into the overall equation and timing within the greater context of the organization. Listen to their advice, but also understand that this is one person who may bring a biased or unfavorable perspective to your overall goal.

Chances are that you are making an ask of someone who has something that you don't—it could be authority, money, resources, influence, and the like. It is highly probable that they may have expertise or knowledge in the area of your need. Be open to feedback, and then run scenarios of possible outcomes.

Check your ego at the door. The only thing you have to lose when asking is by not asking. This is not about your ego, but a chance to engage on a new level of mutual understanding. By asking, you are sharing what is on your mind and perhaps disclosing where your current and future interests lie. Regardless of the outcome, you are moving forward, and that in itself is positive for your goal setting and career path.

You should make your initial ask in a very clear and concise thirty seconds or less. People like to hear themselves talk, but the more they talk and take time away from their ask, the more they dilute what it is they are asking for. A concise, thirty-second pitch is commonly known as an *elevator pitch*, where the pitch should last as long as a typical elevator ride, which is about thirty seconds. According to Princeton psychologists Janine Willis and Alexander Todorov, it takes all of a tenth of a second to form an impression of a stranger from his or her face, and longer exposures don't significantly alter those impressions.[2] Therefore, you want to make those thirty seconds count. An elevator pitch should include the following elements:

- Your goal
- Open with a question
- Your unique selling point (why you are the person to best accomplish this goal)

Follow your elevator pitch with three supporting statements. Be concise and to the point by using three supporting statements that succinctly follow your elevator pitch. For example, you may want to name your company, provide a reputable fact about your company, and say what you are seeking. These three supporting statements will cover the how, why, where, and when and allow the person you are speaking with to think about the various ways they can support your ask or provide a counteroffer. Use a confident, strong voice instead of a submissive vocal tonality—a dominant pitch without hesitation to prove you know what you want.

Make direct eye contact with the person you are asking. This is a simple rule, but one that needs emphasizing in our technology-consumed world. Accordingly to Carol Kinsey Goman, PhD, "We increase eye contact when dealing with people we like, admire, or who have power over us. In more intense or intimate conversations, we naturally look at each another more often and hold that gaze for longer periods of time. In fact, we judge relationships by the amount of eye contact exchanged: the greater the eye contact, the closer the relationship."[3]

Think win-win and expect a "yes." Presenting your pitch is a great opportunity to create a mutually beneficial relationship between you and a colleague. Try to use this time to seek commonality and a shared vision, think of what value you bring to the table, and pose it in a way that is a win/win for you and the company.

In a negotiation presentation made by Jeff Loewenstein, an associate professor of business administration at University of Illinois at Champaign-Urbana, Loewenstein discusses three parts to exchanging a deal: claim, cultivate, and create. According to Loewenstein, "Claiming value is mainly about using power and influence to satisfy our own interests today, whereas the second goal, 'cultivating value,' is about building relationships and reputations and so is more concerned with tomorrow than today."[4] Many times, the value gained from building relationships is far more significant than a single deal. Loewenstein goes on to say, "Do not be misled into believing you're soft if you focus on developing partnerships, because when you're looking long term, like seeking a promotion or a contract renewal, then cultivating value looms larger than claiming it." This relates to the third goal of "creating value." Creating value is about sharing knowledge and figuring out how each individual can help one another.

Go into your session expecting to hear "yes." Winners think that they are going to win—they expect it—and they approach the conversation with a higher energy level than someone who is insecure in the potential outcome.

If you don't close the deal, be sure that you continue the conversation. Follow up within a week of your initial conversation, as that time frame provides ample time to think about how you can reposition your ask, address unanswered questions, and let the receiving individual know that you are serious and committed to what you are asking for. If the answer ends up being "no," ask the recipient to change his or her answer to "Yes, and . . ." and continue to seek new ways to improve upon your ask and build a coalition in support of it. It is important for people and managers to see the value of what you are asking for.

Don't Forget the Offer

One of the very first questions that many people ask in Silicon Valley is, "How can I help you?" This question originally came out of the mouths of very accomplished people who were grateful for the support they got from others before them, but it trickled down, and the question became part of a virtuous cycle, integral to Silicon Valley's innovative success.

At Alley to the Valley, we have an unspoken rule that you have to offer three times before you can ask. You can't ask without thinking about giving. The art of the ask in business should be, "I need this" and "You need that." In other words, "Can you help me?" and "I will help you"—a take and a give. Pay forward, coined by Lily Hardy Hammond in her book *In the Garden of Delight* (1916), is when the beneficiary of a good deed repays it to others instead of to the original helper. In Silicon Valley, paying it forward is one of the region's greatest attributes, and is an integral part of its continued economic success.

Are you offering
the power of hope?

At the Manchester Bidwell Project, a community training and development organization in action, founder Bill Strickland engages during a ceramics class.

THE TRUTH OF TRUST

As Deborah takes her morning run through Los Altos Hills, a Silicon Valley neighborhood of pastoral landscapes where many of the technorati live, she is reminded of the region's past and its future. There is Gordon Moore, who founded Intel and whose namesake is Moore's Law.[1] Around the corner is the estate built by Wilfred Corrigan, a man instrumental in the growth of Fairchild Semiconductor and later founder of LSI Logic Corporation. There is the home of Sergey Brin, the cofounder of Google and current president of Google's parent company, Alphabet, which is leading innovations in the autonomous automobile and Google Glass, among so many other inventions. Then there is the estate of Yuri Milner, the Russian billionaire who was an early investor in Facebook, Twitter, and Groupon and is now investing in a science fiction–like plan to send tiny probes to Alpha Centauri, 4.37 light-years away, via laser propulsion, cutting the interstellar commute from thirty thousand years to about twenty.

Besides extreme wealth, what do these great risk takers have in common? They understand that people, not processes, create great products. They lay out bold moonshots and find the smartest, collaborative people to make genius results happen. They encourage others to think really big, way outside the lines, and share their ideas to explore the unimaginable. They hire people and wait to be told what to do. They leverage the talents, interests, hobbies, and passions of the people they collaborate with. More times than can be recounted here, the results have reaped rewards beyond what anyone could have ever imagined.

Yet outside Silicon Valley's exponentially paced world, the incumbent corporate world is slow to understand what it takes to unleash the potential of their people and unlock hidden growth opportunities. Oddly enough, the incumbents will invest in many things but often bypass their people. Today's leaders finance millions of dollars in technology, management consultants, distribution channels, marketing campaigns, and even art for the office. All of this is easy to account for on the books, but people are not clear-cut; in fact, people are definitively messy.

How do you put a price on the value of a person, the cost of their recruiting, training, ideas, production, execution, and so on? How do you price the opportunities lost when people do not perform to their full potential or use all their creativity? When it comes to people, they are human and dealing with human emotions and the day-to-day events of marriage, kids, death, illness, divorce, parents, friends, enemies, mistakes, triumphs—too messy to manage on a one-to-one level. We have heard the half-hearted words of company leaders who say their people are their greatest assets; if this were really true, why would people seem to get lost in the equation and why would it be that these company leaders manage like they are the most important person in the organization?

The answer lies in the brass ring of *genius*. People are not owned assets. We are living beings with free will. We have feelings, interests, passions, likes, and dislikes. We are both rational and irrational. We both conform and rebel. We will choose to buy something or work more closely with another person because of how we feel. Entire fortunes have been built on connecting with the hearts of others, such as with Harley-Davidson, which has such a passionate, loyal following that the brand has its own owners group, HOGS, that embodies a dedicated community lifestyle for its members.

Genius doesn't follow process (though it can be aided by a democratizing process, such as Improvisational Innovation). Genius comes from the soul, a place that we feel between the head and gut. It is our belief that genius usually starts from a gut feeling that something can change and improve or be created anew. That feeling travels through our minds, making connections with what we know and triggering our imagination of what can be improved or created from scratch. Our gut helps lead us. Our head directs us to the right path to get there. When the gut feels that the idea is right, we act on that idea. We surround ourselves with people who can help us make the idea a reality. If the idea works, the sparks of genius fly.

Nonetheless, companies don't spend time on genius. It can't be measured on quarterly reports. There is no algorithm for gut feelings or imaginations. Leaders are balancing the profit focus of shareholders with the potential brilliance of their workers. And we know who wins that battle most often. We don't need to figure this out, as genius is not a number. We are human, and we don't need to be scientific about any of it.

Genius inspires others. We see Odell Beckham of the New York Giants catch a football with one hand, and millions of children around the country try to emulate this play the next day. Elon Musk redefines the electric car with a sleeker, sports-car model, and we watch the rest of the traditional automotive industry try to follow suit. We will willingly change something in our lives if we are inspired to.

To cultivate genius, you have to treat people like people. In doing so, you have to evaluate your management style. Are you hard-charging or do you baby the people you manage? Do you control their every move and expense? When you are trying to solve problems, are you listening to them even though they may have the lowest paycheck in the room? Are you giving them a safe place to bring new ideas to the table?

If you can spend time to make time for a person's review, then you can set aside time for a person's next project. You can spend time to harness someone's genius. This is a formula to inspire your employee's soul.

We envision a world where people are free to pursue their

passions, work based on their ideas for how to improve, and create. We envision a world where there is respect for people's individuality. Our desire to live in a world like this is not merely because it's a concept that sounds nice or is personally appealing, but because it functions a lot better. History has taught us the perils of oppression and the rewards of hope. The United States was founded on the belief that freedom and hope can create something much greater.

Genius is picking good seeds, good soil, and fertilizer; providing the right environment, light, and food, and then you have the chance to see something amazing bloom. Keep it in the dark or underfeed it, and you end up with something less than you had hoped for. Cross-pollinate with knowledge and collaborate with others, and although you risk failure, you might also see something brand new that has never been seen before, so beautiful that it warms the soul. That is genius.

We spend more time at work in our lifetimes than we do anywhere else, so when we stepped back to thoroughly and thoughtfully examine what the People Equation is, it became quite simple to us—put people first! We leave you with four of our favorite people who embody the People Equation.

Sheldon Yellen:
People Need to Be Taken Care of Like Family

When it comes to doing what is right, Sheldon Yellen trusts his gut. As CEO of BELFOR, a company that provides relief and reconstruction services after fires, earthquakes, hurricanes, and other natural disasters, Sheldon has grown BELFOR from a $5 million construction company to the largest restoration company in the world, with $1.6 billion in revenue. This growth happened all by word of mouth, with his employees providing exceptional service and emotional support to customers. Sheldon provides his people the freedom to become everyday heroes for their customers. Lose a century-old rocking chair in an uncontrolled forest fire, don't be surprised if a new rocking chair is waiting for you when the job is done. Lose your daughter's favorite teddy bear during an evacuation, you might find an employee has tracked you down to hand deliver that bear back to your daughter. Sheldon set up BELFOR to go above and beyond what any work order or invoice documents.

Sheldon trusts his people. He does not hire based on what his bottom line says. He looks at the person. With more than seven thousand employees worldwide, Sheldon has personally met with every potential management hire. Year after year, he personally handwrites birthday cards to every single employee. Sheldon flies out to see the sick children of his workers and wears a wristband for each one. And when times get tough with business, he acts on behalf of his people first.

When the housing market suffered its worst recession in decades in 2007, Sheldon didn't lay off a single employee. He accomplished this by freezing salaries, cutting executive pay by half, and taking substantial personal financial hits. In a January 2011 episode of the CBS series *Undercover Boss*, Sheldon became the first undercover CEO to break from his disguise and reveal himself. He did this after spending hours in a tight, damp, and dirty crawl space with an amazing employee and hearing her story about her severe money issues taking care of her family with no raises. He realized that he had not shared with her or the company why he froze salaries and moved rapidly to rectify things for his people.

In a July 2016 CNBC *Make It* feature, Sheldon shares why so many leaders have their priorities in the wrong place. Yellen says, "You can't show and feel emotion, compassion, passion or intent through a smartphone, through text." While it may seem outdated in a world of continually evolving technology, Sheldon relies on a basic flip phone for communication, encouraging phone conversations with colleagues, clients, friends, and family.

Sheldon's approachable attitude has allowed the CEO of an international company to foster sincere relationships with his employees and their families.

Arlan Hamilton:
Breaking Up the Face of Venture Capital

A few years ago, while working in the music-touring industry, Arlan Hamilton became fascinated with the start-up world and began to lend her ear, advice, and network to several start-up founders and angel investors as a hobby. Helping these entrepreneurs raise capital gave Arlan a rush. Over time, she noticed that there seemed to be an investor "blind spot" to a huge group of innovators who didn't fit the stereotypical founder mold—the "white, male, nerds ... Harvard dropouts" that venture capitalist John Doerr referred to as the type of people he likes to invest in during his keynote at a 2008 National Venture Capital Association meeting.[2] Arlan realized there was an opportunity to capitalize on this, where the "traditional investors loss could be my gain."[3]

There was nothing in Arlan's background that would suggest that she would have a career in venture capital, and she certainly didn't look the part. She was a Silicon Valley outsider, in her early thirties, African American, and gay. She was trying to raise a fund through other venture capitalists, but Arlan insists that in the beginning, she'd get a pat on the head and be told by Silicon Valley notables, "Let's connect later."

Then the day came. Arlan could no longer accept the face of the typical venture capital investor, so she crafted a blog post for Medium called, "Dear White Venture Capitalists: If You're Reading This, It's (Almost) Too Late." The piece went viral. She wrote: "Therefore, if you haven't hired a team of people who are of color, female, and/or LGBT to actively turn over every stone, to scope out every nook and cranny, to pop out of every bush, to find qualified underrepresented founders in this country, you're going to miss out on a lot of money when the rest of the investment world gets it."[4]

The blog post attracted the eyes of Marc Andreessen, one of Silicon Valley's most valued investors. Arlan asked Marc to follow her on Twitter, and the two started to converse on other topics.

In an August 2016 *Inc.* magazine article called, "How This Woman Went from Homelessness to Running a Multimillion-Dollar Venture Fund," Arlan shared that she spent everything she had to bootstrap her mission. For months, she found herself homeless, "sleeping on couches, in motels, out of cars, at airports." Yet Arlan didn't care, because at the end of the day, it was the statistics that drove her. Specifically, a mere twenty-four African American women received venture funding from 2012 to 2014, according to a #ProjectDiane report released in February 2016.[5] She knew she was in this mission for the long haul.

As a weary Arlan sat contemplating her reality, her phone rang. It was Susan Kimberlin, a tech veteran from PayPal and Salesforce, whom she had met at an earlier Y Combinator Female Founders Conference. They bonded over the fact that they believed that diversity was technology's next big gain. "I'm in," Susan said. After a year of fund-raising, Arlan had her first investment in her fund, now called Backstage Capital, exclusively for underrepresented founders—women, people of color, LGBT. After Susan, a string of powerhouse investors followed, including Marc Andreessen; Chris Sacca and his wife, Crystal English; David Rose; Aaron Levie; and Swati Mylavarapu.

Aniyia Williams, CEO for Tinsel, was one of Arlan's first investments. "Last year, when I was raising money, being black, being a woman, being pregnant—it was just strike after strike of what investors are not interested in," said Aniyia, according to the *Inc.* article. "But when I talked to Arlan, she got it right away."[6]

Arlan gets that people will be watching her, more closely scru-tinizing her investments, her returns. "My job is to make money for my investors, and I can't do that with companies based on my heart. It has to be based on companies that are badass."[7]

When Deborah asked Arlan why she had stuck it out and believed she could get a key to the world of venture capital, Arlan stated, "I grew up very quickly understanding that I was going to have to do more if I wanted to be seen as equal. I was going to have to work at least twice as hard if I was even going to be given a chance or taken seriously." [8]

Holly Ruxin:
Impact Investing Isn't Enough,
We Need a New Value System

Holly Ruxin built her career in the global financial system invest-ing client assets at some of Wall Street's most powerful firms: Goldman Sachs, Morgan Stanley, Montgomery Securities, and Bank of America. In the brand names of Wall Street, Holly learned how to play the game and commanded the characteristics she needed to survive: strength, aggressiveness, street smarts. As her role evolved from a derivatives trader to a wealth man-ager, her love of capital markets and investing guided her to sup-port the values, needs, and goals of her clients in the short and long term. Holly had internalized the message to achieve success.

By 2008, Holly was happily living in San Francisco. She had two young children and another on the way. Her life was evolving as she designed it many years before. And then one day, every-thing changed. Her toddler wasn't progressing the way he was "supposed" to. At almost five years of age, her son, Trevor, started missing and then losing all his developmental milestones. He lost his ability to talk, to walk, to use his hands, and to interact with others physically or mentally.

Holly traveled for years to various hospitals and to see lead-ing physicians in their fields, but no one could diagnose what was wrong with Trevor—not the accomplished doctors with Ivy League pedigrees who worked at the top hospitals throughout the country or held chairmanships in top research institutions. Trevor's condition forced Holly to reasses her life.

In chorus, Wall Street was unraveling, and the implications of the financial crisis had begun to deeply impact the global and US economies. Holly's experience with derivatives helped her to understand the catastrophic implications of an opaque market, greed, and the deep misalignment between her values and those of many of her colleagues, people she once respected and admired. Inside her, a voice was growing louder, and she asked herself, "Do people in top positions in our society share my values?"

The answer did not come overnight. After years of thought, observation, and honesty, Holly realized that a new value system was the only way forward. This was a big idea that had several practical implications. She is now the founder and CEO of Montcalm TCR (Tools for Care and Renewal), a wealth-management and capital-markets trading firm guided by the values of integrity, collaboration, engagement, and client sustainability. Montcalm serves as a guiding force for developing a better relationship with money and investing within a new global socioeconomic model that supports the values, needs, and goals of investors. Holly oversees portfolio asset allocation, including internally managed domestic and global fixed income and equities and externally managed alternative investments.

Redeploying assets from an unsustainable financial system requires a global resource shift that cannot be funded by wealthy donors or grant-based programs alone. To create abundance on a massive scale and raise global standards for what constitutes a viable financial life, Holly believes we need investment vehicles that are transparent, liquid, and available in a free market. Imagine a grants program that provides assets such as a cow, access to well water, or fibers for knitting blankets, which has years of data proving that poor families become owners of thriving businesses. Holly's vision is to take the data from these grants, create a structure and framework that shows investors the timing and amount of expected return on investment, and create a security that can be bought and sold as easily as a bond in Apple, Walmart, or Microsoft.

Through her collaboration with the United Nations' Sustainable Development Goals initiative and the United States Global Connect Initiative, Holly is leading the effort to provide creative, capital markets–based financing for projects driving global connectivity. While some people may call this impact *investing*, Holly disagrees with this characterization and believes is it much deeper. To her, *socio* means behaviors of our society and *economics* is a set of processes that lead to a desired effect. Focusing on impact alone allows people to skip over the foundation. We need to ask what are the factors that drive values in our society. Do we believe that investing means creating value and moving our planet toward a better future? According to Holly Ruxin, it does, and she's out to prove to the world that a new business model in investing can be profitable and have noble societal change for the world.

Bill Strickland:
"We're in the hope business.
We manufacture hope."

The video production crew, consisting of more than fifty people, hung on every word William E. Strickland Jr. spoke. Not because he provides a great sound bite, which he does, but because he is someone who truly knows how to move people. The crowd around him barely knows his story and is tasked with the simple job of filming a short commercial for the local hospital, and yet, everyone is rapt by his genuine affect and illuminating sense of compassion; the man can give you goose bumps; he's that inspiring.

He sits down at the potter's wheel and throws a clay pot like it's nothing, his eyes sparkling with effervescent joy. What the video crew doesn't realize is that ceramics for Bill is the truest form of happiness and he hasn't had the strength to do it for almost two years due to advanced chronic obstructive pulmonary disease. He is now five months post-op, having undergone a double lung transplant. Thus, it is only fitting that all eyes are on him as he returns to the place where he found his own North Star and where his story began.

Bill should have been just another statistic. Growing up in Pittsburgh, he was besieged by racism in the crumbling remains of the steel economy. A resident of the inner city Manchester neighborhood during the civil-rights era, he was, by his own admission, detached from his life. He never thought of the future because dreams were for those who could afford them.

Entering his senior year of high school with failing grades, Bill was intrigued by an art teacher whose classroom he casually passed one day. That teacher, Frank Ross, was throwing clay pots and listening to jazz music. Frank simply looked up from his work and said, "Can I help you, son?" It was the first time anyone had shown an interest in him.

Bill couldn't take his eyes off the potter's wheel and its magical movement. He was completely invested from the moment he saw the clay begin to take shape and found in it a new sense of purpose. Frank began mentoring Bill, and his support was instrumental in eradicating the teen's apathy. As a result, Bill went on to earn a bachelor's degree in American history and foreign relations from the University of Pittsburgh, graduating cum laude in 1969.

However, while attending college, Bill wasn't content simply working to sell his ceramics and becoming a respected local artist. Particularly following the assassination of Dr. Martin Luther King, Jr., Bill saw an increased need for hope within his community. He encountered countless kids struggling to survive the urban decay and who felt there was no way out for them. Bill knew firsthand what they were experiencing and he felt compelled to open their eyes, just as Frank had done for him.

Bill believed then, and continues to believe to this day, that people are assets, not liabilities, and that the way you treat them is what drives their performance and behavior. People can be born into all sorts of circumstances, but we are all deserving of beauty, light, and hope.

Prior to his graduation from college, Bill founded Manchester Craftsmen's Guild (MCG) to bring arts education and mentorship to the youth of his neighborhood. Forty-eight years later, the program serves approximately 3,900 youths each year through classes and workshops in ceramics, photography, laboratory and pharmacy technicians, digital imaging and design, and culinary art, among other fields. MCG Arts gives students a chance to work intensively with visiting artists of national and international stature through exhibitions, lectures, workshops, residencies, and school visits. Now 98 percent of MCG's students graduate from high school on time.

In addition, Bill has since developed several national and international social enterprises under the Manchester Bidwell Corporation umbrella, ranging from a Grammy award–winning record label and jazz concert series to an adult career training center and a 40,000 square foot wholesale greenhouse. But his greatest contribution is his ability to spread his message that hope heals. In fact, Bill has been dubbed the "Hopemaker."

"When welfare mothers come into our place, tired from the couple of bus rides it took to get here, they find themselves resting on pieces of art. I want our students to get comfortable with art. I want them to be confronted by something beautiful every time they turn around," says Bill.[9]

Bill has now taken his educational model and push for hope in difficult times to ten cities around the country and the Middle East with his Akko Center for Arts and Technology, which opened in November 2016. He believes the programming provided based on the Manchester Bidwell Corporation will not only empower the local population but also bridge the divide among Jews and Arabs.

And while the Pittsburgh film crew hangs on his every word, there's no doubt that he'll make it, because Bill has an unwavering hope and faith in all people, no matter what condition they were born into. "I have discovered a cure for our spiritual cancer," says Bill. By providing people with both the tools they need to succeed and the things that will make them happy and inspire them to work, people thrive. Bill has an unfailing commitment to give disadvantaged people the very best and has spared no expense when it comes to his facilities and educational programs because he knows that people of low socioeconomic means are often dehumanized and get the message early on that they have no future or their lives don't matter—specifically, that what they see around them is all that they deserve. "Life is real, it's not just an idea," says Bill.[10]

Go and Inspire Your People

We've collaborated on a joint vision for innovative effectiveness, ever since our first conversation at the Robotics Hacker Dojo in Mountain View, California in the summer of 2011. Deborah was fascinated with the Montessori-style problem solving that David had created at the dojo, where teams of people could collaborate and individuals could generate breakthrough thinking by poring over a box kit that simply offered a problem to solve that was part of a greater whole. Deborah thought, "What if every company had a dojo to solve problems and inspire people to think big?"

Both of us came from hierarchical, bureaucratic environments where people were not really part of the equation. Yet, it took living through these—sometimes abrasive—environments to arrive at another way, a better way. We can now guide the organizations we work into a future that is kindler and gentler, but provides the path to growth that companies are going to need to survive and flourish.

Just like people we admire with strong convictions, so too do companies need convictions and a culture, so that people inside and out of the company understand what they stand for. They need a culture where people are not micromanaged and commanded and controlled, but where people are treated like family, to be able to be at their very best, to help raise the company from infancy to adulthood.

Our conversation that day at the dojo and the many conversations that followed became the precursor to this book. It seems clear that the future that sits before us all will doubtless change more quickly than at any time in history; there will be greater uncertainty, greater risk, and greater rewards for all of us. In this future, it behooves us to focus on and inspire our people— because that is the only way that we can confront an uncertain future with the certainty that together we will succeed.

NOTES

Introduction

1. Michael Chui, James Manyika, and Mehdi Miremadi, "Where Machines Could Replace Humans—and Where They Can't (Yet)," *McKinsey Quarterly*, July 2016.

2. Frederick Winslow Taylor, *The Principles of Scientific Management* (New York: Harper & Brothers, 1911).

3. ibid., 9.

4. Patrick Viguerie, Sven Smit, and Mehrdad Baghai, *The Granularity of Growth: How to Identify the Sources of Growth and Drive Enduring Company Performance* (New York: Wiley, 2008).

5. Tim Brown, *Change by Design: How Design Thinking Transforms Organizations and Inspires Innovation* (New York: HarperCollins, 2009).

6. McKinsey & Company, "Innovation and Commercialization 2010: McKinsey Global Survey Results," August 2010, http://www .mckinsey.com/business-functions/strategy-and-corporate-finance/ our-insights/innovation-and-commercialization-2010-mckinsey- global-survey-results.

7. Jason Furman and Peter Orszag, "A Firm-Level Perspective on the Role of Rents in the Rise in Inequality," presented at A Just Society: Centennial Event in Honor of Joseph Stiglitz, Columbia University, October 16, 2015, https://www.whitehouse.gov/sites/default/files/ page/files/20151016_firm_level_perspective_on_role_of_rents_in_ inequality.pdf.

8. McKinsey & Company, " Growth & Innovation," accessed November 5, 2016, http://www.mckinsey.com/business-functions/strategy-and- corporate-finance/how-we-help-clients/growth-and-innovation.

9. ROIC is a common metric of financial performance. It is an important factor in the creation of shareholder value.

10. Steve Denning, email to authors, April 2016.

11. Larry Kim, "10 Critical Skills You'll Need to Succeed at Work in 2020," *Inc.*, May 27, 2015, http://www.inc.com/larry-kim/10-critical- skills-you-ll-need-to-succeed-at-work-in-2020.html.

12. Deborah Perry Piscione, *Secrets of Silicon Valley: What Everyone Else Can Learn from the Innovation Capital of the World* (New York: St Martin's Press, 2013).

Chapter 1, The Psychology of Innovation

1. Karl Duncker, "On Problem Solving," *Psychological Monographs* 58, American Psychological Association. OCLC 968793.

2. Uri Gneezy, Stephen Meier, and Pedro Rey-Biel, "When and Why Incentives (Don't) Work to Modify Behavior," *Journal of Economic Perspectives* 25, no. 4 (Fall 2011): 191–210.

3. See Sanjiv Erat and Uri Gneezy, "Incentives for Creativity," *Experimental Economics* 19, no. 2 (June 2016): 269-80; Colin F. Camerer and Robin M. Hogarth, "The Effects of Financial Incentives in Experiments: A Review and Capital-Labor-Production Framework," *Journal of Risk and Uncertainty* 19, no. 1 (December 1999): 7–42; and Pierre Azoulay, Joshua S. Graff Zivin, and Gustavo Manso, "Incentives and Creativity: Evidence from the Academic Life Sciences," *The RAND Journal of Economics* 42, no. 3 (Fall 2011): 527–54.

4. See W. A. Kahn, "Psychological Conditions of Personal Engagement and Disengagement at Work," *Academy of Management Journal* 33, no. 4 (December 1990): 692–724; Markus Baer and Michael Frese, "Innovation Is Not Enough: Climates for Initiative and Psychological Safety, Process Innovations and Firm Performance," *Journal of Organizational Behavior* 24, no. 1 (February 2003): 45-68; Abraham Carmeli, Jane E. Dutton, and Daphna Brueller, "Learning Behaviours in the Workplace: The Role of High-Quality Interpersonal Relationships and Psychological Safety," *Systems Research and Behavioral Science* 26 (2009): 81–98; Amy C. Edmondson "Managing the Risk of Learning: Psychological Safety in Work Teams," in *International Handbook of Organizational Teamwork,* ed. Michael West, Dean Tjosvold, and Ken Smith (London: Blackwell Publishing, 2003); Amy C. Edmondson, "Psychological Safety, Trust, and Learning in Organizations: A Group-Level Lens," in *Trust and Distrust in Organizations: Dilemmas and Approaches,* ed. Roderick Kramer and Karen S Cook (New York: Russell Sage Foundation, 2004), 239–72; Douglas R. May, Richard L. Gilson, and Lynn M. Harter, "The Psychological Conditions of Meaningfulness, Safety and Availability and the Engagement of the Human Spirit at Work," *Journal of Occupational and Organizational Psychology* 77, no. 1 (March 2004): 11–37.

5. Edmondson, "Managing the Risk of Learning."

6. Emily J. Hanna, "Exploring the Relationship Between Reporting Medication Errors and Nurse Fear of Retribution," Graham-Webb University, Hunt School of Nursing, 2014.

7. Nathaniel Rich, "The Risky Appeal of Free Climbing," *The Atlantic*, November, 2015.

8. Guy Kelly, "How to Become the World's Most Fearless Climber," *The Telegraph*, May 9, 2015, http://www.telegraph.co.uk/men/active/ 11592972/How-to-become-the-worlds-most-fearless-climber.html.

9. Edmondson, "Psychological Safety."

Chapter 2, The Process: Improvisational Innovation

1. Pat Younge, email to authors, April 24, 2016.

2. Andrew Martin, *How to Get Things Really Flat: A Man's Guide to Ironing, Dusting and Other Household Arts* (London: Short Books, 2008).

3. "iCreate Wins One Show Commission," last modified August 2, 2013, accessed November 10, 2016, http://www.bbc.co.uk/ariel/23547390.

4. Deborah Perry Piscione, *The Risk Factor* (New York: St. Martin's Press, 2014).

5. Cirque Du Soleil, "About Us," accessed November 4, 2016, https:// www.cirquedusoleil.com/en/home/%20%20about-us/at-a-glance.aspx.

6. Isaac Asimov, "Isaac Asimov Asks, 'How Do People Get New Ideas?,'" *MIT Technology Review*, October 24, 2014, https://www .technologyreview.com/s/531911/isaac-asimov-asks-how-do-people- get-new-ideas/.

Chapter 3, The Inverted Organization

1. Quotations in this section are from interviews conducted by David Crawley.

2. Quotations in this section are from interviews conducted by the authors.

3. Brandon Rigoni and Bailey Nelson, "Do Employees Really Know What's Expected of Them?," *Gallup Business Journal*, September 27, 2016, http://www.gallup.com/businessjournal/195803/employees- really-know-expected.aspx.

4. Stephen Heyman, "Big-Box Bookstores Don't Have to Die," *Slate*, December 15, 2015, www.slate.com/articles/business/moneybox/

2015/12/barnes_noble_is_dying_waterstones_in_the_u_k_is_thriving
.html.

5. Marvin Bower, *The Will to Manage: Corporate Success Through Pro-grammed Management* (New York: McGraw-Hill, 1966), 7.

Chapter 4, Risk-Taking Leadership

1. Saurabh Gupta, interview with the authors, n.d.

2. David Maister, Charles Greene, and Robert Galford, *The Trust Advisor* (New York: Free Press, 2002).

3. James P. Womack, Daniel T. Jones, and Daniel Roos, *The Machine That Changed The World* (New York: Free Press), 119.

Chapter 5, The Corporate Culture of How

1. Robert Safian, "Terri Kelly, the 'Un-CEO' of W. L Gore, On How to Deal with Chaos: Grow Up," *FastCompany*, October 29, 2012, https://www.fastcompany.com/3002493/terri-kelly-un-ceo-wl-gore-how-deal-chaos-grow.

2. Daniel Cable, Francesca Gino, and Brad Staats, "Breaking Them In or Eliciting Their Best? Reframing Socialization around Newcomers' Authentic Self-Expression," *Administrative Science Quarterly* 58, no. 1 (March 2013): 1–36.

3. See John Stachel et al., eds. *The Collected Papers of Albert Einstein*, vol. 1 (Princeton, NJ: Princeton University Press, 1987–2006), 11; and Albrecht Fölsing, *Albert Einstein: A Biography,* trans. Ewald Osers (New York: Penguin Viking, 1998).

4. Laszlo Gyorffy, interview with the authors, February 28, 2016.

Chapter 6, It Only Takes One

1. Herbert Spencer, *The Study of Sociology* (1873).

2. Steve Jobs, commencement address, Stanford University, Stanford, CA, June 12, 2005.

Chapter 7, Moving beyond the Comfort Zone

1. "How the ARM1 Got Built by Steve Furber," ElectronicsWeekly.com, May 14, 2007, http://www.electronicsweekly.com/blogs/mannerisms/yarns/how-arm1-got-built-by-steve-fu-2007-05/.

2. Jacob Sachs, phone interview with the authors, April 2015.

3. "Cost to Develop and Win Marketing Approval for a New Drug Is $2.6 Billion," Tufts Center for the Study of Drug Development, November 18, 2014, http://csdd.tufts.edu/news/complete_story/pr_tufts_csdd_2014_cost_study.

Chapter 8, The Art of the Ask

1. Pamela Ryckman, "The Risk-Taking Edge of West Coast Women," *New York Times,* November 10, 2010.

2. Chad Boutin, "Snap Judgments Decide a Face's Character, Psychologist Finds," News at Princeton, August 22, 2006, https://www.princeton.edu/main/news/archive/S15/62/69K40/index.xml?section=topstories.

3. See Goman's book *The Silent Language of Leaders: How Body Language Can Help — or Hurt — How You Lead* (San Francisco: Jossey-Bass, 2011).

4. See Loewenstein's website at http://business.illinois.edu/loewenstein/.

Epilogue: The Truth of Trust

1. Moore's law is the principle that the number of transistors on integrated circuits has doubled roughly every eighteen months since the days of the first integrated circuits.

2. Sam Colt, "John Doerr: The Greatest Tech Entrepreneurs Are 'White, Male, Nerds,'" *Business Insider,* March 4, 2015, http://www.businessinsider.com/john-doerr-the-greatest-tech-entrepreneurs-are-white-male-nerds-2015-3.

3. Arlan Hamilton, phone conversation with the authors, August 18, 2016.

4. Arlan Hamilton, "Dear White Venture Capitalists: If You're Reading This, It's (Almost!) Too Late," *Medium,* June 13, 2015, https://medium.com/female-founders/dear-white-venture-capitalists-if-you-re-not-actively-searching-for-and-seeding-qualified-4f382f6fd4a7#.ynr1wuqfg.

5. Kathryn Finney and Marlo Rencher, *The Real Unicorns of Tech: Black Women Founders,* #ProjectDiane report, February 2016.

6. Salvador Rodrigues, "How This Woman Went from Homelessness to Running a Multimillion-Dollar Venture Fund," *Inc.*, August 12, 2016, http://www.inc.com/salvador-rodriguez/arlan-hamilton-backstage-capital.html.

7. Ibid.

8. Phone conversation with authors, August 16, 2016.

9. Bill Strickland, with Vince Rause, *Make the Impossible Possible: One Man's Crusade to Inspire Others to Dream Bigger and Achieve the Extraordinary* (New York: Broadway Books), 13.

10. Quoted in commercial filmed by University of Pittsburgh Medical Center for Manchester Bidwell Corporation, September 25, 2016.

ACKNOWLEDGMENTS

We owe a debt of gratitude to so many wonderful people, but we first want to acknowledge how we met, through Deborah's young son, Dominick, who attended a few sessions of David's robotics events at the Hacker Dojo in Mountain View back in 2012. At one Saturday session, a mutual acquaintance, Vivek Agrawal, and his son Rohan Agrawal, decided to introduce us. Quickly, we realized this kindred spirit for people and innovation, to dream big and know that anything is possible when you collaborate with smart people who are steadfastly willing to say yes when you ask them to chip in.

This book would not have been possible without our agent, Wendy Keller, who was so diligent in her tenacity and very convincingly suggested that we work with Berrett-Koehler as our publisher, due to their highly collaborative process in book publishing. So much thanks goes to our editor, Neal Maillet, who helped massage this book into the important message it advocates.

To our equally enthusiastic innovation brethren, we'd like to thank Laszlo Gyorffy, Dr. Lisa Freidman, and Herman Gyr, who were always willing to jump in to lend an ear, an imperative anecdote, or a great debate on the status quo and the future.

To Phillip Farah, who took countless time out of his work and family schedule to provide a strong critique of the content and structure of the book. To Karen Tucker, the CEO of the Churchill Club, who is always willing to make a meaningful introduction.

To Deborah's speaking agent, Michael Humphrey, of NextUp, who would provide the most stimulating fodder over today's business culture.

To Sam Metcalf for taking the time to share in detail the operations of CRM as well as provide additional literature.

To Sam Hyde for taking the time to describe the rich simplicity of the mindset at The Technology Partnership (TTP) as well as being the ideal role model of it.

To John Shook for showing David that the Lean system is as much about attitude as it is systems, and to Durward Sobek for teaching us what true Lean product development is.

To Abi Graham and Colin Crawley for invaluable input and guidance on some of the specific case studies.

To our families—without their support, this book would not be possible.

INDEX

ABOUT THE AUTHORS

 **Deborah Perry Piscione** is a serial entre- preneur, thought leader in innovation processes, and the author of four books, including the *New York Times* best seller *Secrets of Silicon Valley*. A frequent speaker on innovation, Deborah teaches her orig- inal methodology, Improvisational Inno- vation, in addition to the characteristics of Silicon Valley's ecosystem and culture, to captivated audiences around the world.

Breaking from her roots in tech and content, Deborah is lead- ing her latest entrepreneurial venture, Nobiyo Freshwear, patent- pending retail undergarments that manage perspiration and odor.

She is also the creator of Alley to the Valley (A2V), a nation- wide community of highly accomplished women for the pur- poses of deal flow and deal making. Deborah brings A2V into corporations to facilitate the development of cohesive communi- ties among female executives, where women speak strategically to one another about specific ways to help each other advance, which often yields higher revenue for the firms.

Deborah is the subject of a Stanford University case study, "Deborah Perry Piscione," about finding opportunity in Silicon Valley. Prior to her move to Silicon Valley, Deborah spent eigh- teen years in Washington, DC, working as an on-air commentator for CNN, MSNBC, and Fox News and serving as a congressional staffer on Capitol Hill and an political appointee in the White House of President George H. W. Bush. She lives in Silicon Val- ley with her husband and three children.

 **Dr. David Crawley** is a principal at Vorto Consulting and specializes in innovation processes, Lean methods, and disruptive change. David is known around the world for his work in transforming and short-ening product-development processes. He led a change process at Cypress Semicon-ductor that reduced lead time from 326 weeks to 17 weeks. He is sought after as a lecturer and speaker.

As a former consultant at McKinsey & Company, David served four of the top-ten semiconductor companies on operational and strategic topics as well as many other companies in the Fortune 500. He holds four patents and numerous highly cited peer-reviewed publications.

David founded Ubiquity Robotics, a community-led group that used Lean methods and Improvisational Innovation to build a novel, high-function robotics platform with a bill of materials cost below $500, based on open source software.

David is an athlete who competed internationally and was an Olympic trialist in rowing in preparation for the 2004 Olympics in Athens, Greece. In addition, David earned a commission from the Royal Military Academy Sandhurst, earned his PhD in physics from the University of Cambridge, and was a postdoctoral fellow at Cambridge University, Clare Hall.

Deborah and David can be reached at their respective emails:

Deborah@vortoconsulting.com
David@vortoconsulting.com

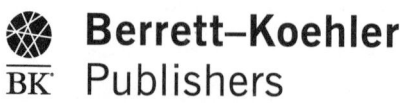

Berrett–Koehler
Publishers

Connecting people and ideas
to create a world that works for all

Dear Reader,

Thank you for picking up this book and joining our worldwide community
of Berrett-Koehler readers. We share ideas that bring positive change into
people's lives, organizations, and society.

To welcome you, we'd like to offer you a free e-book. You can pick from
among twelve of our bestselling books by entering the promotional code
BKP92E here: http://www.bkconnection.com/welcome.

When you claim your free e-book, we'll also send you a copy of our e-news-
letter, the *BK Communiqué*. Although you're free to unsubscribe, there are
many benefits to sticking around. In every issue of our newsletter you'll find

- A free e-book
- Tips from famous authors
- Discounts on spotlight titles
- Hilarious insider publishing news
- A chance to win a prize for answering a riddle

Best of all, our readers tell us, "Your newsletter is the only one I actually
read." So claim your gift today, and please stay in touch!

Sincerely,

Charlotte Ashlock
Steward of the BK Website

Questions? Comments? Contact me at bkcommunity@bkpub.com.

MIX
Paper from
responsible sources
FSC® C002589

Certified

Corporation
bcorporation.net